HOW TO BE A
BETTER CYCLIST
THE ESSENTIAL GUIDE

"The benefits of cycling greatly outweigh the risks – even more so, if you learn to cycle skilfully."

A testimonial from the author

Most people who cycle gain great pleasure from doing so and that certainly applies to me. Cycling is very much a 'doing' activity, where you are actively involved in every inch you move. Modern cycles are designed and manufactured using the latest technology, but balancing, steering and moving a bike are still entirely down to personal effort and not the output of an automated process. In an age where there is so much uniformity, cycling will always be an activity where the individual is all important.

Cycling is also an activity with many myths and misunderstandings. A cyclist may not have the protective shell of a motorist in a car (which means that you are closer to the world about you and your senses can function as intended), but that does not have to mean that you are less safe. The fact that people who cycle regularly live longer, on average, than people who do not cycle, with less ill-health, says it all. The benefits of cycling greatly outweigh the risks, and all the more so if you take the trouble to learn to cycle skilfully.

A key message is that most bad driving and other hazards can be anticipated and their effects avoided. While statistics show that other road users are often to blame for crashes involving adult cyclists, in most cases the cyclist could have avoided the incident entirely by riding more diligently.

I welcome the initiative of the IAM to include cycling in the activities for which they offer sound advice and I have been pleased to be involved in the production of this book.

My own interest in advanced cycling started with entirely selfish motives. I wanted my cycling to be less physically demanding, safer and able to take me wherever I wanted to go. So I spoke to people who had these skills and experimented with different techniques until I found what worked best.

One outcome is *How To Be A Better Cyclist*, which incorporates many of the same principles that also underpin the IAM Advanced Driving and Advanced Motorcycling programmes. As a result, I am confident this book will give you a head-start in your own quest to become an advanced cyclist.

Good luck, and enjoy your cycling!

John Franklin
Cycling Skills and Safety Consultant
Author of *Cyclecraft*

© 2010 the IAM.
How To Be A Better Cyclist is published by the Institute of Advanced Motorists in conjunction with madaboutmedia.com

Words by John Franklin
Photography and production by John Sootheran
Designed by Mark Guest
Reprographics by AT Graphics
Printed in the UK
ISBN 978-0-9562239-2-0
With thanks to Duncan Pickering

HOW TO BE A BETTER CYCLIST
THE ESSENTIAL GUIDE

Experience the pleasure of cycling safely and efficiently

HOW TO USE THIS BOOK

This book should be used for self-study and to supplement advice you may receive from a National Standards cycling course. The way it is organised allows you to find the relevant subjects and advice quickly and easily under general headings. The most important aspects of *How To Be A Better Cyclist* are summarised at the end of each of the major topics in a Rider Checklist.

PREREQUISITES

How To Be A Better Cyclist assumes that you can already ride a bicycle and that you have acquired the basic skills of bike control and riding in some traffic. If you lack these skills, or wish to teach the basics to someone else, such as a family member, you are referred to *Cyclecraft* for more information.

CONTENTS

HOW TO BE A BETTER CYCLIST - THE ESSENTIAL GUIDE

4 Testimonial from the author
5 How to use this book
  Prerequisites
8 What advanced cycling is about
  Go on, get involved
10 Hazards on the road
12 Cycling basics
  Your cycle and you
  Your state of mind
  Avoid cycling if you…
13 Always room for improvement
  Your reaction time
  Other people's reactions
14 Types of bike
16 Maintenance check list

1 PREPARING TO RIDE

19 Clothing and equipment
  Cycling commuter
20 Public transport commuter
21 Enthusiast
  Shopper
22 Riding position
23 How to check for blind spots
  Should you wear a helmet?

2 BASIC PRINCIPLES OF ADVANCED CYCLING

24 Hazards
25 Why you need to think ahead
26 Planned system of cycling
  A good instinct to have
  Time to react
  IPSGA
27 IPSGA applied to a right turn
28 The importance of IPSGA
30 Observation

31 Forward observation
  Rear observation and checking
  for blind spots
32 Selective observation
34 Road signs
  Road sign rules
36 Riding plans
  Three simple questions
38 Positioning
  Standard riding positions
39 Overtaking a parked car
  Moving to the primary position
40 Turning
  Forward vision
41 In town
  Country bends
42 Conservation of momentum
43 Plan ahead
44 Braking
  Bicycle brakes in action
45 Skidding
  Braking distance
  Overall stopping distance
46 Forward clearance
  Emergency braking
47 Brake failure
48 Changing gear
  Why use gears?
  Changing gear

3 RIDING TECHNIQUES IN ACTION

50 Road basics
  Junctions
51 IPSGA applied to a left turn
52 IPSGA applied to turning
  right at a roundabout
53 Roundabouts
  Mini-roundabouts
54 Signalling at roundabouts
56 Turning right at crossroads
  (off the major route)
  Crossroads and T junctions
57 Traffic lights

58 Negotiation
   Establishing cooperation
59 Overtaking by negotiation
60 Turning right by negotiation
62 Negotiation at roundabouts
64 Cycling in town
   Extra demands of town
   cycling
65 Route observation in town
   Filtering
66 Observation and 'stepping
   stones'
67 Common errors when filtering
68 Undertaking
69 Road surfaces in town
70 Bus lanes
71 Confidence in congested
   conditions
72 Cycle facilities
   Cycle lanes
73 Cycle paths next to the road
74 Reactions of other drivers
   Other cycle facilities
75 Cycling in the countryside
   Main roads
76 Country lanes

77 Climbing hills
   Descending hills
78 The 'Limit Point of Vision'
79 Cattle grids and fords
   Horses
80 Cycling in tricky conditions
   Cycling at night
81 The advantages of
   night cycling
   Dazzle
82 Cycling when it's windy
   Rain
   Fog and mist

83 Riding when it's cold
84 Cycling in summer
86 Roadworks
   Roadworks
87 Diversions
88 Cycling for the family
89 Sharing a parent's bike
90 Riding alone
91 Cycling with children
92 Advanced Riding Index
94 Thank you
95 Other IAM products
   and services
96 Notes

What advanced cycling is about

- Being in total control… all of the time
- Developing observation, anticipation, positioning and timing at junctions and roundabouts, so that you can integrate into traffic with ease and confidence
- Understanding what you are doing and why
- Anticipating the behaviour of other road users
- Becoming a thinking rider, not an automaton
- Minimising effort, so cycling is a pleasurable experience

GO ON, GET INVOLVED

By reading this book and showing an interest in advanced cycling, you're well on the way to improving your cycling ability.

Advanced cycling involves acquiring skills and confidence, and by studying this book and applying what you learn from it, you WILL become a better, safer rider.

You'll learn to ride with greater precision and awareness, anticipate hazards created by other road users' mistakes and allow a big enough safety margin to avoid getting into trouble. You don't need to ride submissively, always worrying about your vulnerability to motor traffic. Instead, you will plan dynamically – always as appropriate to the circumstances – in a confident and decisive manner. This way you will always make good progress with minimum physical effort.

Hazards on the

Each time you cycle on the road, you face a whole host of potential
this picture - it highlights the sort of risks you could face in your

BEING SEEN.
Cycles are small and
may be overlooked
in the mayhem of
traffic. Emphasise
your presence by positioning
yourself prominently.

**WORN/UNEVEN ROAD
SURFACES.**
Potholes, ridges,
raised manholes and
poorly reinstated trenches are
hazards that you need to avoid.

road

hazards. Check out
everyday cycling

DISTRACTED DRIVERS. Drivers on the phone, fiddling with their sat-nav or talking to passengers are less likely to notice a cyclist.

IMPATIENT AND LAZY DRIVERS. Excessive speed, road-rage, poor lane discipline and late braking are all behaviours you must allow for.

OTHER HAZARDS

- tired drivers
- drivers with poor eyesight
- unsignalled manoeuvres
- low, blinding sunlight
- unfavourable gradient
- wet and slippery surfaces

These are just a few of the hazards you'll discover on Britain's roads. Advanced cycling prepares you to deal with all of them.

Cycling basics

Keeping yourself, and your cycle, in good condition is essential if you want to get the most out of cycling

YOUR CYCLE AND YOU

Your safety depends on the condition of your cycle. Spend just five minutes a week checking your machine's brakes, gears and transmission system (the parts linked together by the chain), tyre pressures and wear, and lights. This will maintain your safety and also get the best performance and reliability from your cycle.

Your state of mind

When cycling on busy roads, it's important to always be in the right frame of mind.

Positive, tolerant and courteous attitudes reduce the risk of collisions, as do being realistic about your own abilities and maintaining a high degree of care for your own, and others', safety.

Cycling on congested roads can be very stressful, so always aim to remain cool-headed and courteous – helping to diffuse threatening situations, or avoiding them altogether.

Don't let your standards be affected by other people's mistakes or behaviour, and remember that, if you make a mistake, an apologetic wave is often all it takes to put things right.

Avoid cycling if you...
- Are feeling tired.
- Have flu or feel unwell.
- Are stressed or feel aggressive after, say, a bad day at work or a row at home. Also if you are elated or over-excited about something.
- Have consumed drugs or alcohol. Even some mild medicines, such as cold treatments, may make you feel drowsy.

The laws about alcohol consumption apply as much to cyclists as to motorists. It is preferable to avoid drinking altogether before cycling. Also, never listen to music or a mobile phone, and avoid using headphones when you are cycling. Hearing is one of the most important senses for a cyclist and you may miss important signals about impending hazards if you are distracted.

Don't let your enthusiasm for cycling tempt you into taking chances or riding in an unsafe way. Always aim to ride decisively and display a high level of self-control, planning each manoeuvre as you progress.

ALWAYS ROOM FOR IMPROVEMENT

No matter how long you've been cycling, there's always room to improve your cycling skills.

Keep an open mind, be realistic about your limitations and always be prepared to learn from any errors you make.

YOUR REACTION TIME

Your thinking distance varies with the speed of your machine, your physical and mental condition and the degree of concentration applied. Even with lightning reflexes, the distance your cycle covers before you apply the brakes can be considerable, to which must then be added the braking distance itself. Your reactions slow when you are tired, cold, ill or stressed. Drugs and drink have a negative impact too, but may actually make you think you're reacting more quickly than normal.

If you suspect imminent danger ahead, position your hands over the brake levers. In towns and on busy roads, you should ride in this way most of the time. This will save valuable milliseconds if you need to slow down or stop.

The diagram below shows the distances you'll cover in the time it takes to react (not brake) at 15, 20 and 25mph. With this in mind, always allow yourself plenty of time and space.

REACTION DISTANCES

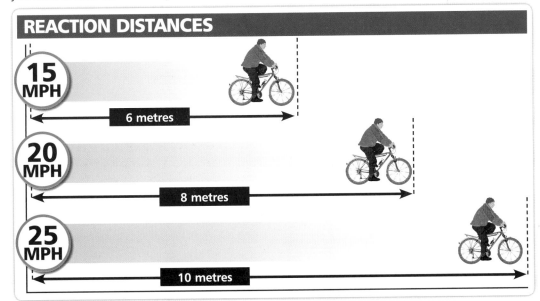

15 MPH — 6 metres

20 MPH — 8 metres

25 MPH — 10 metres

OTHER PEOPLE'S REACTIONS

Always expect the worst from other road users. If you allow for poor observation and slow reactions, you'll find you're always prepared for the worst-case scenario.

Don't ride too close to a vehicle in front – it will probably be able to stop more quickly than you.

"Always expect the worst from other road users."

TYPES OF BICYCLE

HYBRID BIKE

A cross between a road bike and a mountain bike. This is the best choice for most people, suitable for riding about town and for limited off-road use and short-distance leisure cycling. Derailleur gears and brakes are sturdy and easy to use, and full mudguards and a pannier rack are useful for everyday journeys. Hybrids can be lightweight and efficient, especially when a suspension system isn't fitted.

SMALL-WHEEL BICYCLES

These are manoeuvrable and stable and can be easily adapted in size to a number of users. However, most are inefficient and suitable only for cycling short distances.

CITY BIKE

Robust machines with the emphasis on on-road cycling for short trips. An angled handlebar, upright riding position and hub gears make for machines that are durable, if a little heavy.

FOLDING BIKES

Available in several wheel sizes, these are useful for commuting by public transport. More expensive models are versatile and suitable for many cycling purposes.

ELECTRICALLY-ASSISTED CYCLES

Useful for older people and others with disabilities, especially if they live in a hilly area. These machines are heavier and less responsive than an ordinary cycle, so you may have to carry out many manoeuvres more cautiously.

TANDEMS

A great way for two people to cycle together, especially if one rider is stronger than the other.
Also a useful way to introduce children (who ride as the stoker on the back) to cycling in traffic.

MOUNTAIN BIKE

The broad tyres, numerous gears and robust suspension systems of a mountain bike are great for use off-road, but less good on-road, where these cycles are sluggish and less manoeuvrable. Not ideal for most uses.

SPORTS, ROAD OR TOURING CYCLE

With a diamond frame, dropped handlebars and high-pressure tyres, these bikes feature excellent manoeuvrability and are ideal for integrating with traffic. The best choice for longer-distance touring, they work well for commuting too.

TRICYCLES

Ideal for carrying shopping and children, as well as for people who cannot balance well on a bicycle. They are very stable machines, but less manoeuvrable where roads are congested.

RECUMBENT CYCLES

The 'laid back' position of the recumbent rider is good for people with back or neck problems. These comfortable machines are available as solos, tandems and tricycles.

MAINTENANCE CHECKLIST

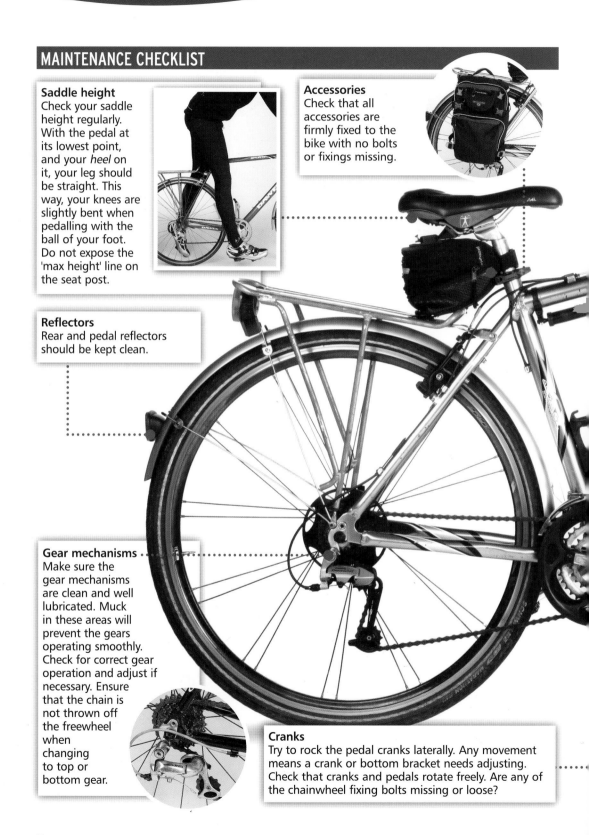

Saddle height
Check your saddle height regularly. With the pedal at its lowest point, and your *heel* on it, your leg should be straight. This way, your knees are slightly bent when pedalling with the ball of your foot. Do not expose the 'max height' line on the seat post.

Accessories
Check that all accessories are firmly fixed to the bike with no bolts or fixings missing.

Reflectors
Rear and pedal reflectors should be kept clean.

Gear mechanisms
Make sure the gear mechanisms are clean and well lubricated. Muck in these areas will prevent the gears operating smoothly. Check for correct gear operation and adjust if necessary. Ensure that the chain is not thrown off the freewheel when changing to top or bottom gear.

Cranks
Try to rock the pedal cranks laterally. Any movement means a crank or bottom bracket needs adjusting. Check that cranks and pedals rotate freely. Are any of the chainwheel fixing bolts missing or loose?

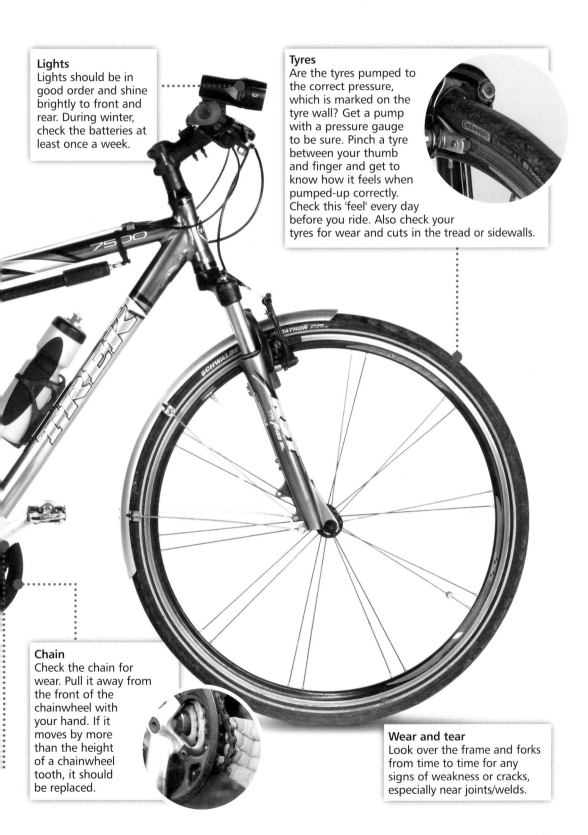

Lights
Lights should be in good order and shine brightly to front and rear. During winter, check the batteries at least once a week.

Tyres
Are the tyres pumped to the correct pressure, which is marked on the tyre wall? Get a pump with a pressure gauge to be sure. Pinch a tyre between your thumb and finger and get to know how it feels when pumped-up correctly. Check this 'feel' every day before you ride. Also check your tyres for wear and cuts in the tread or sidewalls.

Chain
Check the chain for wear. Pull it away from the front of the chainwheel with your hand. If it moves by more than the height of a chainwheel tooth, it should be replaced.

Wear and tear
Look over the frame and forks from time to time for any signs of weakness or cracks, especially near joints/welds.

MAINTENANCE CHECKLIST

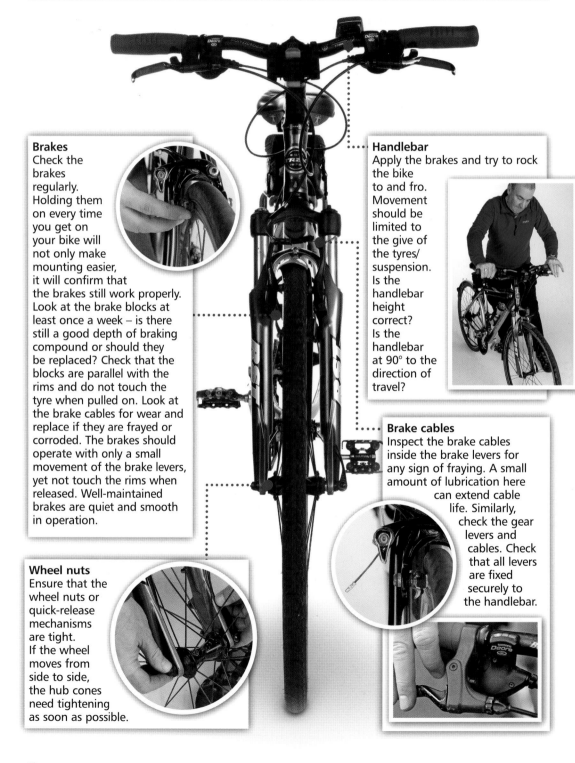

Brakes
Check the brakes regularly. Holding them on every time you get on your bike will not only make mounting easier, it will confirm that the brakes still work properly. Look at the brake blocks at least once a week – is there still a good depth of braking compound or should they be replaced? Check that the blocks are parallel with the rims and do not touch the tyre when pulled on. Look at the brake cables for wear and replace if they are frayed or corroded. The brakes should operate with only a small movement of the brake levers, yet not touch the rims when released. Well-maintained brakes are quiet and smooth in operation.

Handlebar
Apply the brakes and try to rock the bike to and fro. Movement should be limited to the give of the tyres/suspension. Is the handlebar height correct? Is the handlebar at 90° to the direction of travel?

Brake cables
Inspect the brake cables inside the brake levers for any sign of fraying. A small amount of lubrication here can extend cable life. Similarly, check the gear levers and cables. Check that all levers are fixed securely to the handlebar.

Wheel nuts
Ensure that the wheel nuts or quick-release mechanisms are tight. If the wheel moves from side to side, the hub cones need tightening as soon as possible.

Clothing and equipment

Choose the right apparel and gear for comfortable, efficient cycling

As an energetic activity, cycling warms you when it's cold, while the draught you generate cools you when it's hot. The main requirement for clothing when cycling is that it should be light and loose fitting. If you're riding a short distance, everyday clothing is fine, but for longer or faster rides, specialist cycling clothes are more comfortable.

Here are four cycling scenarios, though clothing and equipment are not restricted to a particular cycling purpose.

CYCLING COMMUTER

Waterproof garments
Buy cycling-wear that is water and wind-proof, but that is breathable to keep you dry.

Visibility
Light-coloured garments are always best, and high-visibility clothing is most easily seen in dense traffic, particularly in poor weather.

Luggage
Always aim to carry luggage on the bike, not on your back.

Toe clips
These keep your feet on the pedals, enabling quicker starts and increasing pedalling efficiency.

Cycling shoes
They can make pedalling easier and will keep your feet dry.

How to be a better cyclist

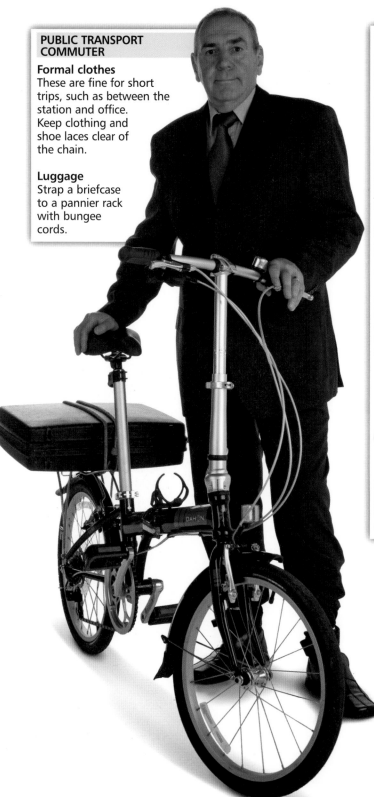

Formal clothes
These are fine for short trips, such as between the station and office. Keep clothing and shoe laces clear of the chain.

Luggage
Strap a briefcase to a pannier rack with bungee cords.

ENTHUSIAST

Helmet
Helmets may absorb minor impacts, but are not proven to offer effective protection in more serious crashes, such as those involving motor vehicles.

Shorts/tights and jersey
Padded shorts or tights prevent saddle soreness, while cycling jerseys allow sweat to escape, keeping you dry and comfortable.

Specialist cycling shoes with clipless pedals
These slot together for easier, more efficient pedalling.

Gloves or mitts
Keep hands warm and absorb handlebar vibration, while allowing easy operation of the brakes.

Visor
Useful for keeping insects and rain out of your eyes.

SHOPPER

Everyday clothes
Fine for short distances, but avoid flared trousers, long skirts and long laces that may get caught in the chain/gear mechanism. Shoes should not have deep treads or smooth soles.

Luggage
A front basket is fine for light loads, but for shopping, or anything heavy, use pannier bags for better balance.

ALSO REQUIRED

- Good quality lock
- Full-length mudguards for road use
- Pump and toolkit
- Front and rear lights

Riding position

Achieving the best riding position is essential for the advanced cyclist. Here's how to do it...

The correct position for a cyclist allows excellent control over your bicycle, maximum comfort and enhanced alertness, even on long journeys.

Sit on the saddle and place the *heel* of one foot on its pedal, with the pedal crank extended in line with your leg. The saddle should be set in height so that your leg is straight at the knee. When you ride normally, with the ball of your foot on the pedal, your knee will be slightly bent. If you sit on the saddle with one foot on its pedal, the other foot should be able to reach the ground and support you comfortably, whilst offering good stability. This may not be possible with some bikes. If that is the case, you should start and stop the bike off the saddle.

Reach out to the handlebar so that you can grip it comfortably, with your hands over the brake levers. You should be neither too stretched nor cramped when you do this. You should be able to operate the brake and gear levers easily.

Your posture and other bike adjustments vary according to the style of cycle. Seek advice, if necessary, to ensure that it is the correct size and properly adjusted for you.

HOW TO CHECK FOR BLIND SPOTS

Ask someone to walk slowly behind you from side to side and note the points at which they disappear from view, then reappear. Between these points is your blind zone. Be aware of this and compensate by looking more carefully and allowing for hazards in this 'invisible' area.

Your blind zone can be decreased or eliminated by turning at the waist as well as turning your head. This takes more time to do, so ensure that you have sufficient clear distance ahead to complete this movement safely.

Before any manoeuvre you make, consider taking a quick look over your shoulder to check that you haven't missed anything in the blind spot.

SHOULD YOU WEAR A HELMET?

Cycle helmets are optional and not a legal requirement. Although the IAM does not discourage any cyclist from wearing one, it is important to be aware of certain facts.

Statistically, the risk of serious head injury when cycling is very low – similar to that for a car occupant and less than the risk to a pedestrian. The fact that cyclists live longer, on average, than people who do not cycle, suggests that cyclists are not at special risk of any life-threatening injury.

Helmets protect well against low-impact knocks and scratches, but are much less effective in high-impact crashes, such as those involving motor vehicles.

Your best defence against injury when cycling is to avoid conflict altogether by riding diligently and skilfully. The means of realising this are the subject of this book.

> **RIDER CHECKLIST**
> ● Maintain your cycle regularly and keep it safe to use.
> ● Ensure that it is always adjusted to suit you correctly.
> ● Be properly dressed for the conditions and type of cycling you plan to do.

2 // BASIC PRINCIPLES OF ADVANCED CYCLING

Hazards

The UK's busy roads are filled with potential dangers. Learn to spot these hazards and take appropriate action

In busy urban traffic, hazards are all around. The advanced cyclist has the anticipation, vision and skill to cope with all of them

A hazard is anything that contains an element of actual or potential danger. This includes: road narrowings, junctions, roundabouts and bends, as well as the position and movement of other road users. The weather can also be a hazard. Imagine combining several of these elements in one scenario, and you have great potential for something to go wrong. Hazards can exist at any roundabout, traffic lights or turn, not just where a child runs into the street or there is a blind bend or accident black spot. It is essential to position your bicycle correctly to deal with hazards, giving you that essential ingredient, sufficient time to react, to avoid them.

Imagine almost any crash situation; if you had sufficient warning you would almost certainly be able to avoid it. This is the cornerstone of a planned system of cycling.

⚠️ One of the most commonly-occurring hazards is a parked car. Identify this hazard, and position yourself appropriately, well before you reach it. Assume the 'primary position' (p38) to dominate your side of the road, otherwise you may be forced to brake and lose all your momentum.

WHY YOU NEED TO THINK AHEAD

On pages 10 and 11 we showed you just some of the potential hazards you could face every time you ride your bicycle. To minimise your chances of being affected by adverse riding conditions or other people's mistakes, you need to take a planned and systematic approach to your riding. This means you'll anticipate hazards, spot them earlier and allow enough time and space to avoid them all together. Even in the worst-case scenario, you'll give yourself enough time to take effective evasive action.

Thinking ahead means that every manoeuvre is made in good time and under control.

Keep a close eye on parked traffic for signs that it may be intending to pull out

These images show how easy it is to misread the road ahead, especially when travelling at speed. Here the road appears to go left, so you won't expect traffic appearing from the right, especially if it's coming fast.

Don't feel pressured to rush your decision-making because of impatient traffic behind. You are entitled to obstruct traffic, where it would not be safe for it to pass

A planned system

A GOOD INSTINCT TO HAVE

Cycling in a systematic way is especially beneficial in difficult riding situations. It lets you manage hazards in a calm, planned, efficient and flexible manner.

The early recognition of hazards such as physical features, the position and movement of other road users, changes in road surface and the weather, gives you time to plan your progress instinctively.

TIME TO REACT

Road features such as roundabouts and junctions can be hazardous. Generally, they're easy to deal with, but can be complicated by their layout, the movement of other road users, poor road surfaces and bad weather.

These more difficult situations require the use of a planned cycling system, which gives you time to assess and react appropriately. The IPSGA system was developed for motorists and motorcyclists for this exact purpose, and has now been adapted for use by cyclists.

INFORMATION

Absorb Information: Be aware of what's going on all around you, including behind.
Process Information: On the basis of your observations, plan how to deal effectively with the hazards that you have identified.
Give Information: If you are going to cross the path of other traffic (or pedestrians), always give a clear hand signal before you move. There are other times, too, when a signal can be helpful to other road users and you should give one if it is safe to do so.

POSITION

Position your cycle on the road to maximise your safety and to minimise the amount of physical effort you need to provide. Check first that you have sufficient space to move into.

SPEED

Decide on the speed that is required for the manoeuvre that you intend to make. You may need to accelerate in order to be able to integrate with traffic, or you may need to slow down in response to a hazard ahead. In other cases, you may not need to alter your speed at all. To slow down, freewheel if you can, using the brakes only when necessary.

GEAR

If you need to accelerate, consider changing to a higher gear in order to achieve this. If only a short burst of acceleration is required, it may be sufficient to alter your cadence (the rate at which you turn the pedals). If you need to slow down or stop, changing to a lower gear will make subsequent acceleration or restarting easier.

ACCELERATION

If you had to slow down, accelerate back to your riding speed after the hazard. If you increased speed to integrate with traffic, ease off pedalling. Change gear as necessary to achieve your optimum cadence.

IPSGA can be applied to any cycling manoeuvre. While it may appear longwinded, with practice it will become the natural thing to do.

It is intended to be used in sequence, with the Information element (in red above) overlapping the other three.

If circumstances alter, restart IPSGA at the appropriate point. All aspects should be consciously considered, not just applied slavishly.

As well as raising awareness of what's going on around you, IPSGA also ensures that your actions won't take other road users by surprise.

That said, you should still keep an eye on other road users to make sure that they have seen you and are acting as you would expect them to.

# of cycling

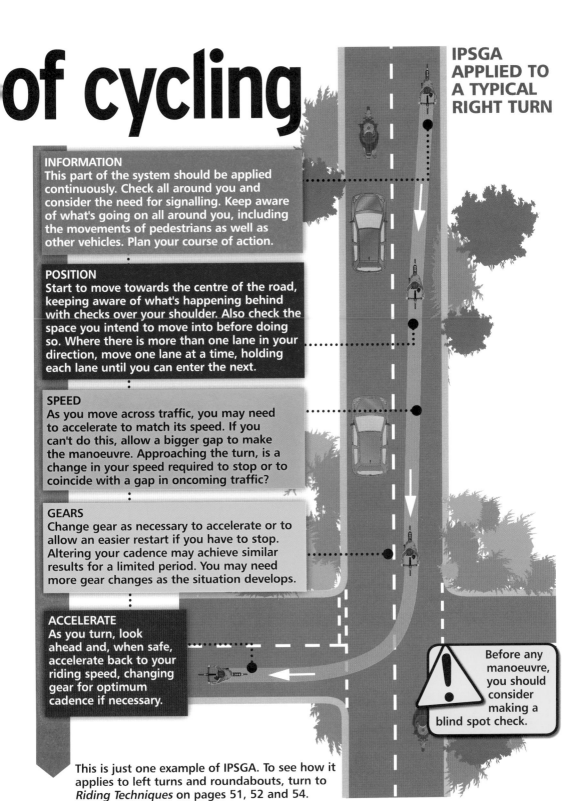

INFORMATION
This part of the system should be applied continuously. Check all around you and consider the need for signalling. Keep aware of what's going on all around you, including the movements of pedestrians as well as other vehicles. Plan your course of action.

POSITION
Start to move towards the centre of the road, keeping aware of what's happening behind with checks over your shoulder. Also check the space you intend to move into before doing so. Where there is more than one lane in your direction, move one lane at a time, holding each lane until you can enter the next.

SPEED
As you move across traffic, you may need to accelerate to match its speed. If you can't do this, allow a bigger gap to make the manoeuvre. Approaching the turn, is a change in your speed required to stop or to coincide with a gap in oncoming traffic?

GEARS
Change gear as necessary to accelerate or to allow an easier restart if you have to stop. Altering your cadence may achieve similar results for a limited period. You may need more gear changes as the situation develops.

ACCELERATE
As you turn, look ahead and, when safe, accelerate back to your riding speed, changing gear for optimum cadence if necessary.

Before any manoeuvre, you should consider making a blind spot check.

This is just one example of IPSGA. To see how it applies to left turns and roundabouts, turn to *Riding Techniques* on pages 51, 52 and 54.

THE IMPORTANCE OF IPSGA

Practise the IPSGA system regularly and it will soon become second nature. Once you do it instinctively, you'll have more time to concentrate on other aspects of your cycling.

Planned IPSGA cycling has many benefits, including enhanced safety, less stress and more economical riding.

Know what is going on around you at all times and let others know what you intend to do. This effective absorption, processing and giving of information is essential to better cycling.

Plan your approach to every hazard. Consider freewheeling so that vehicles ahead move on before you arrive.

Think about what you can see, but also what might be hidden from you. You aren't going to miss a brightly-coloured truck, but what about the motorcyclist tucked in behind it?

Early planning and good positioning let you have control over your safety in the most difficult circumstances.

Plan your approach to every junction. Aim to time your arrival so that you don't have to stop in this vulnerable position between fast-moving lanes of traffic.

Absorbing and processing information throughout any manoeuvre is essential. A slow-moving tractor and trailer won't be missed, but the impatient driver behind may not see you when he darts out for his overtaking manoeuvre.

Early planning and good positioning let you have control over your safety on the approach to a junction, making for a safer ride.

To restart quickly if you have to stop, keep one foot on its pedal and move this to the two o'clock position (viewed from the right side of the bike). Toeclips or clipless pedals make this much easier.

On most bikes, you cannot change gear when you are stationary. Ensure that you select the correct gear for restarting before you come to a complete standstill.

RIDER CHECKLIST
- Use the planned system of riding (IPSGA) every time the traffic situation changes.
- Track the movement of vehicles behind you by glancing over your shoulder.
- Check that there is free space to move into before you attempt to change position.
- Signal before you cross the path of other traffic or pedestrians. Signal at other times when it is helpful to others and safe to do so.
- Plan your application of the system to suit the prevailing circumstances.

Observation

Perfecting your vision and observation will help to keep you safe on the roads. But improving your observation skills takes commitment, consideration and lots of practice

Some threats are very obvious. It's the ones that aren't that you need to be alert to, like this junction obscured by a bus shelter, bin and bollards

Effective observation is a crucial element of advanced cycling. It gives you the time to plan ahead and spot potential hazards before they become a serious problem.

To improve your riding, you must try to absorb as much information as possible every time you cycle. There are dozens of things going on at any given moment and you have to quickly process all that information, focusing on things that are relevant, and disregarding those that are not. Of course, everyone does this to a degree, but develop this skill and you can take your cycling to another level entirely.

Constantly assess riding conditions, read the road as far ahead as you can and make decisions accordingly.

Poor eyesight can affect reaction times and spatial awareness, while restricted peripheral vision may cause you to completely miss a hazard. Most people's eyesight deteriorates very gradually as they get older. It's a good idea to have an eye test every two years or whenever you suspect there's been a deterioration in your vision. Always heed an optician's advice regarding wearing spectacles or contact lenses for cycling.

FORWARD OBSERVATION

Many people only focus on the road just ahead of them. This means they may have insufficient time to react to any hazards they meet. Cyclists are vulnerable to road surface defects as well as traffic, so they need to be particularly vigilant in observing conditions ahead of them. The more warning you have of hazards, the easier they are to deal with.

The key is to constantly scan the area closest to you, as well as looking into the middle distance and all the way to the horizon. When you look ahead, you will still be aware of what is happening close to you. However, concentrating on the near-ground, often means you'll miss warnings further ahead.

Every time the view ahead of you changes – when you turn a corner, round a bend or reach the crest of a hill, for example – scan again. This early-warning system allows you to identify approaching hazards, spot potentially dangerous drivers and gives notice of traffic hold-ups and road works.

Many ordinary riders have a very narrow field of vision...

...while advanced riders take in information from all around them

REAR OBSERVATION AND CHECKING FOR BLIND SPOTS

Check the situation behind you regularly, especially in busy traffic

Rear observation involves being aware of what is going on behind you by looking over your shoulder. You will not see the same level of detail that you see ahead, but you should know what types of vehicles are behind, how far away they are and their approximate speed. Aim to engage eye contact with the driver behind if you can, as this ensures they are aware of your presence.

You must be able to turn your head sufficiently to do these checks, while gripping the handlebar with both hands and holding a straight course. Don't look behind if there is a vehicle just ahead that might brake.

Most of the time, you will need to look over your right shoulder, but you should always glance behind to the left before moving or turning left, to ensure another cyclist or motorcyclist will not try to come past you on the inside.

Rearward observation to both the left and the right can be important at roundabouts.

It is also useful to be able to look further behind by turning at the waist. This can increase the notice following drivers take of you and allow you to get more detailed information. To do this, you must remove one hand from the handlebar on the side you will be looking, making sure you have a much greater safe-distance ahead.

As with every other part of IPSGA, when you look behind should be determined by your riding plan for the prevailing circumstances, and not just undertaken slavishly.

SELECTIVE OBSERVATION

Good observation is crucial to advanced cycling. Riders with effective observation skills have to process lots of information quickly, so it's essential to develop a way of instantly distinguishing between useful and less relevant information. Here are some useful tips:

● Has the driver emerging at the junction ahead seen you, and is he going to give way? If you're unsure, move to the centre of your lane, first observing traffic behind and ahead. Be prepared to brake if it becomes necessary.

● Look out for changes in the colour or texture of the road surface ahead. This often gives warning of surface hazards that you may need to avoid.

● Potholes, reinstated trenches, manhole covers, drains and any other changes in the surface ahead. Avoid these hazards if you can, by changing your position, or be prepared for a less comfortable ride by keeping firm (but relaxed) control of the steering and lifting your weight from the saddle. Pointing to a continuing hazard can help to

make other drivers aware of your predicament.

● Watch pedestrians carefully, especially children and anyone walking a dog. Don't assume everyone can see and hear you, and look for people moving between parked vehicles.

- Always be prepared to react to the unexpected.
- A build up of traffic or a cluster of lamp posts ahead may give warning of a roundabout or major junction.
- In busy, urban environments, use shop window reflections to observe approaching vehicles or changing traffic lights before you can see them directly.

At night, similar reflections can provide reassurance that your lights are in good order.

- Observe parked vehicles ahead. Make preparations to move out, well clear of any doors that might open. If there are occupants or the engine is running (look for exhaust fumes and lights), consider that the vehicle might suddenly pull out in front of you.

- Pay extra attention to stationary vans where the driver might be concentrating on making a delivery. Give them a wide berth.
- When travelling behind a bus, be aware that when passengers start moving around inside, it's likely that a bus stop is coming up. Prepare to overtake if it's safe to do so. Dropping back a little as the bus slows can make this easier. Always pass buses, school transport and ice cream vans cautiously, in case children

attempt to cross the road in the shadow of the vehicle.

- As you approach a large or slow vehicle coming towards you, be aware that impatient drivers may attempt to overtake it without noticing or making any allowance for your presence.
- Observe the actions of other road users. If they're acting in a risky, distracted or aggressive way, keep your distance.
- Look through breaks in hedges and fences to spot approaching vehicles.
- At night, use other vehicles' headlight beams to assess their whereabouts, direction of travel and speed.

Headlamp beams may also give useful information about the course and surface of the road you are on.

Road signs

Road signs are important aids to knowing what's ahead. Make sure you know what all road signs mean by reading the *Highway Code*

ROAD SIGN RULES

Warning signs are triangular, advisory signs are rectangular and round signs with a red rim are 'the law' – you must do what they say.

Blue signs with white symbols are used to indicate special facilities for cyclists and pedestrians.

You should quickly interpret the signs you see, so that you can keep your attention on the road ahead, looking out for what has been indicated. It is the message that is important, not the sign! If there are two or more signs on a pole, read from the top. On the sign below, you can see that the first bend comes before the junction.

A road junction can have many signs. You need to notice them all and understand quickly what they mean

RIDER CHECKLIST

- Develop your subjective observation and learn to prioritise the information you receive. What information should you act on and what can you ignore?
- Read and understand the meaning of every road sign.
- Keep track of traffic both ahead and behind. Look over your shoulder from time to time, so that you know what's happening behind you.
- Watch the traffic several vehicles ahead. This will give you early warning of potential hazards, hold-ups and general traffic movements.
- Scan continually between the road surface and the traffic; from what lies just in front to as far as you can see.
- Get your eyes tested every two years or the moment you suspect any deterioration in your vision.

Riding plans

Riding plans are a key element of the IPSGA system. How you assess what's going on around you, and how you act on that information is pivotal in taking your cycling to the next level

RIDING PLANS: THREE SIMPLE QUESTIONS

Don't let an unusual manouevre by one road user, distract you from maintaining your all-round vision

What can't be seen? A hidden roadsign can distract as you try to see the warning

What can be seen?
Plan your cycle ride on what you can see ahead, to the rear, and all around you.

What cannot be seen?
Remember that hazards can exist on every hidden section of road: in concealed junctions, driveways, around the next bend or behind another vehicle.

What might reasonably be expected to happen?
Keep a look-out for clues to hazards that may lay ahead:
● Junction signs give notice that a driver may be waiting to pull out ahead or a driver may overtake you and then turn in.

● Loose hedge clippings or straw on a country road warn that there could be farm vehicles round the bend and should also make you consider carefully where you ride so that your tyres don't suffer a puncture from thorns.
● At night, a car's headlight beams will provide plenty of warning of its arrival.
● Will the dump truck behind you overtake and then turn into a construction site? Is it overloaded and could something fall off into your path? Will there be mud on the road?
● Is the bus you can see ahead

What might reasonably be expected to happen? One of these school children could run out at any second

about to pull over at a bus stop? If it is, keep back so that you will not have to move out so tightly to overtake it.

- Always be aware that other drivers could (and probably will) do something totally unexpected at any moment.
- Prioritise hazards in order of importance and deal with each one accordingly.

With these potential hazards in mind, always ride within the limits of what you can see. Advanced cyclists make no assumptions and are always alert for the unexpected. Their constant planning ahead and highly-tuned anticipation skills ensure that they always have a 'Plan B', should the worst-case scenario become a reality.

RIDER CHECKLIST
- Plan your ride dynamically as you go. Assess your observations and act on them.
- Observe others and allow for their inadequacies. Anticipate and plan for their actions.
- Allow for your own and other people's reaction and braking times in varying riding conditions.
- Ride positively and display courtesy to others whenever you can.

Positioning

Positioning is one of the least-known cycling skills, but it is one of the most important when it comes to cyclist safety

It is through the position a cyclist takes on the road, that they have the most influence over their own safety.

The aims of good positioning are to ride where you can best see and be seen, where you deter or prevent others from putting you at risk, and where control of your cycle is as easy as possible. This chapter explains how to do it.

Ride in the centre of the traffic lane if it is not safe for you to be passed

STANDARD RIDING POSITIONS

You should ride in the primary riding position – the centre of the leftmost traffic lane for the direction you are going – in the following situations: when you can keep up with traffic; when you need to emphasise your presence to drivers behind or ahead; or when you need to deter following drivers from overtaking you because it is not safe for them to do so.

The primary position is where you are most easily seen by other drivers. Hold this position until you're sure it's safe for you to ride further left.

When it is safe to allow other drivers to pass you, ride in the secondary position, about one metre to the left of the moving traffic lane, that part of the road where through-traffic is moving. Note that this position should always be determined relative to the position of traffic, not the kerb. Do not slavishly ride close to the kerb where other drivers may not easily notice you. In any event, never ride closer than 0.5m to the road edge as this will leave you with insufficient 'escape room' in an emergency.

In deciding where to ride, always take into consideration the nature of the road surface. Where the surface is poor, allow yourself extra space in which to divert by keeping further out, indicating, if necessary, to other drivers the need to do this by pointing at the surface defect.

Sometimes, other drivers may suggest that you are in their way and should move, most likely because they do not understand why cyclists often need to ride prominently in traffic. Maintain your position until it is safe for you to move, but be ready to divert quickly if someone acts aggressively.

MOVING TO THE PRIMARY RIDING POSITION

3) In the primary position, it is more obvious to a following driver that there is not sufficient space to overtake

2) After checking the traffic situation behind, he starts to move to the primary position. There's no need to signal unless there's a vehicle close behind

1) Approaching in the secondary position, the cyclist sees a traffic island ahead that will reduce the lane width. He needs to protect himself from being squeezed at this point

This diagram shows how to change traffic lanes to overtake a parked car, or similar obstruction. The bottom cyclist is progressing into the 'Primary Riding Position', the top cyclist is returning to the 'Secondary Riding Position'

TURNING

When turning into or out of a junction or entrance, position yourself prominently so that other drivers do not try to overtake you during the manoeuvre. Usually this will mean adopting the primary riding position. Maintain this position after turning until you are sure that it is safe for you to be overtaken.

"Obscured near-side road junctions can hide a hazard"

Position yourself prominently at the approach to any junction

Dominating your lane like this, deters impatient drivers from cutting you up or undertaking you

FORWARD VISION

When traffic conditions permit, use your position on the road to see more easily what lies ahead and in this way obtain more information. This makes planning more effective.

Obscured nearside junctions (above) can hide approaching vehicles. The further a cyclist is from the road edge, the more easily they will be able to see into the junction and the sooner an approaching driver will see them.

Should the unexpected occur, the cyclist is also further from a potential conflict, and therefore has more time to react.

On approaching a 'T' junction with restricted vision, many drivers will give themselves only a fraction of a second to see if it is clear to drive onto the major road. In addition, they will probably be looking for another car, not a bike. By riding where a car would be driven, you are more likely to

be seen and not obscured by parked cars, trees, pedestrians or hedgerows.

Most crashes involving a cyclist and a motor vehicle occur at junctions. With effective planning and good road positioning – keeping well away from the hazard zone of give-way markings to your side – a cyclist can go a long way towards eliminating the likelihood of these crashes occurring altogether.

Rearward observation is important before you move across the road

In town, hazards tend to come together and your road position is crucial to your safety.

Positioning needs to take account of all the hazards arising at any given moment. You need to prioritise the most important of these dangers, so that you can be sure of staying a safe distance from them as they develop. This gives you the maximum time to react to the most serious hazards, if it becomes necessary.

Always adopt a position to maximise your safety.

COUNTRY BENDS

Position your bike towards the outside of a bend for the furthest and best view through it. This allows you more time to react to hazards and gives an oncoming driver the earliest warning of your presence.

If there are no vehicles on your side of the road (or if there are, but it's unsafe for them to pass you), move towards the right side of the lane approaching a left-hand bend and the left side for a right-hand bend. If moving right, don't ride too close to the centre line.

On single-track roads, make full use of the whole road width to maximise visibility.

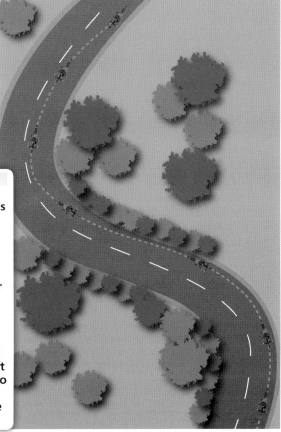

RIDER CHECKLIST
● Place yourself where you can best see and be seen, taking into account ALL that is going on around you.
● When you need to emphasise your presence to drivers behind or ahead, or when it might be unsafe for someone to overtake you, ride prominently in the primary riding position. Remain vigilant for drivers who attempt to pass regardless.
● Always position yourself relative to moving traffic, not the kerb.
● When turning at junctions, adopt the primary riding position to deter other road users from overtaking you. Move to the left after turning, only when it is safe for you to be passed.
● Always take account of the nature of the road surface when deciding where to ride.

Conservation of momentum

A cyclist provides all the power for moving along from personal energy. That's a good reason not to waste it

Momentum is built up every time a cyclist turns the pedals and the faster they go, the greater their momentum.

Having reached any particular speed, momentum helps to propel you forward with less effort than would be required if you had to start from standstill again. When you brake, however, momentum is lost, dissipated wastefully in heat between the brake blocks and wheel rims instead of helping you to move. The conservation of momentum is a key skill for the advanced cyclist, getting the most movement out of every bit of energy you expend.

The principle is to maintain your momentum, by being sufficiently aware of conditions ahead that you can compensate for them by changing your speed, rather than by stopping and restarting. Usually this will mean slowing down a little, which you do by freewheeling or by using a lower cadence (pedalling more slowly).
In this way, you can arrive at a roundabout after another vehicle has passed so you do not have to give way.

If you need to slow down over a longer distance, perhaps because the traffic lights you are approaching have just changed to red, it is more efficient to change to a lower

gear than to alter your cadence. This gives the added advantage that you will be better prepared for stopping and restarting should it become necessary.

Sometimes a burst of acceleration can be a better way to conserve momentum. If you are so close to traffic signals when they change to amber, that to stop would require hard braking, rapid acceleration may get you past the stop line before the red shows and allow you to keep going through the junction.

The primary position protects you from traffic behind and allows you to concentrate on the best time to enter a junction

Slowing down or accelerating to arrive during a suitable gap in traffic will conserve momentum and energy

PLAN AHEAD

If you see traffic ahead starting to slow, or a pedestrian who is about to cross the road, ease off pedalling straight away and make the best use of the momentum you already have.

Use your brakes as little as possible and, when you do use them, apply them with no more force than you have to. As well as maintaining momentum longer (which gives you the opportunity to change to pedalling once more,

should conditions change), this will reduce brake block wear, be kinder to your bicycle and conserve your energy levels.

Another place to think ahead, is when approaching a tight bend or when you intend to turn left. You will need to limit your speed while turning in order to stay in control of the bike, and this should be as a result of a smooth transition from your approach speed, without braking.

RIDER CHECKLIST
- Plan ahead to maintain your momentum.
- Use your brakes as little as possible.
- Slow down or accelerate to avoid stopping when it is possible to do so.
- Consider freewheeling or changing to a lower gear to reduce speed.
- Make all movements smoothly, with gentle transitions when your speed needs to change.

Braking

Bicycle brakes have limited force and rapid braking can destabilise a bike. Taking the time to understand how your brakes work and to develop a smooth, effective braking technique makes every ride safer and more comfortable

BICYCLE BRAKES IN ACTION

Most bicycles have two brakes, one acting on the front wheel, the other on the rear. The most important is the front brake but, if used too harshly, the cycle may pivot about the front wheel and you could be thrown over the handlebar.

The rear brake, used alone, will stop a bike safely but not very quickly. Used together with the front brake, it provides a means of detecting when the bike is about to pivot. This occurs soon after the onset of skidding at the back, which

should be a warning to release braking pressure a little to keep the bike under control. With practice, this becomes intuitive.

To stop a bike safely, you should always apply both brakes, the rear brake a fraction of a second before the front.

SKIDDING

A rear-wheel skid is quite easy to control; a skid at the front, almost impossible. Luckily, front wheel skids are rare, as the rider's weight keeps the front wheel firmly on the ground. However, they can happen on slippery surfaces like ice, leaves, spilt diesel or loose gravel, or if you turn while you brake.

In these conditions, ride more slowly so you don't need to stop as quickly.

Whenever possible, brake only when steering straight.

BRAKING DISTANCE

Total stopping distance is worked out by adding 'thinking distance' and 'braking distance' together.

The time it takes you to react is the main factor in 'thinking distance'. 'Braking distance' will vary according to your speed, the road surface, the condition of your brakes and whether the wheel rims and brake blocks are dry. Wet conditions significantly increase braking distances – the more so the faster you are going.

"Wet conditions significantly increase braking distances – the more so the faster you are going."

OVERALL STOPPING DISTANCE (THINKING DISTANCE + BRAKING DISTANCE)

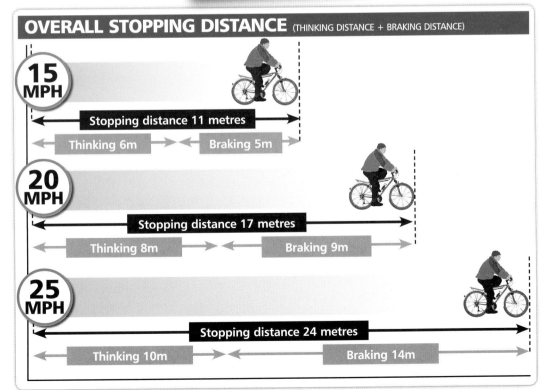

15 MPH
Stopping distance 11 metres
Thinking 6m → Braking 5m

20 MPH
Stopping distance 17 metres
Thinking 8m → Braking 9m

25 MPH
Stopping distance 24 metres
Thinking 10m → Braking 14m

FORWARD CLEARANCE

When you can keep up with traffic, stay a sufficient distance from the vehicle in front so that if it brakes suddenly you do not ride into it. Increase this distance when it is wet.

In slow-moving traffic, cycle in the primary position to dominate the lane and deter drivers behind from leapfrogging you to fill the gap in front.

Staying back not only means you're safe if the driver in front brakes, but enables you to see more of the road ahead

EMERGENCY BRAKING

Looking ahead and anticipating the actions of other people will make the need to brake quickly a rare event. Sometimes a burst of acceleration can be used to get you past the path of another vehicle to better effect. But you will brake more effectively in an emergency if you have practised what to do.

To stop quickly, brake hard with the front brake but apply only normal pressure to the rear brake. As you brake, throw your weight back in the saddle. This will reduce the braking distance and improve your stability greatly.

On most bicycles, straightening your arms is an effective way to move your body weight back. Bracing yourself also maintains good control over direction of travel.

BRAKE FAILURE

Cycle brakes are not as robust as those fitted to motor vehicles, and you should be prepared to deal with brake failure. The most common reason for the braking mechanism to fail is the snapping of a brake cable, usually where it enters the brake lever. Applying lubrication here from time to time will help prolong cable life. The brakes, levers and cables should be inspected for wear often – but check them immediately if you've had to brake very hard.

If brake failure occurs, bring the bike to a halt as quickly as possible with the other brake, but don't pull on it so sharply that it also snaps.

If you are going fast or downhill and there is no other traffic about, zig-zagging cautiously across the road can help you reduce speed. In wet weather, cycle brakes always act more slowly, and in a storm you can prevent a situation developing where the brakes won't work at all by keeping the brakes applied lightly. Aim to prevent the build-up of water on the rim so that there is less to penetrate when you need to slow down or stop.

Brake checks are quick and easy to carry out.

Ensure the brake blocks are aligned with the rim and that the gap between the two isn't more than a few millimetres

Adjust the brakes so that you don't have to pull the brake levers too far

Before every ride, check to see that your brakes are working correctly

---

RIDER CHECKLIST
- Apply your brakes every time you get on your bike, so that you know they are in good working order.
- Allow for your reactions and those of other drivers when you brake.
- Get to know the 'feel' of your brakes and ensure that this remains constant over time.
- Conserve momentum by braking only when necessary. Do not brake sharply unless you have no choice.
- Avoid braking when you are not travelling in a straight line.

Changing gear

Using gears correctly, minimises the effort required to cycle and improves your ability to integrate with traffic

WHY USE GEARS?

Gears match the energy you provide as a rider with the power requirements of your bicycle. These requirements vary with acceleration, terrain and wind resistance.

As all the power required to move a bicycle comes from its rider, gears enable you to make the most efficient use of your muscles, making cycling more comfortable. When people say they find cycling hard work, it is almost invariably because they are not using the gears correctly.

Each person has his or her own optimum cadence, or rate of pedalling. You use gears in order to maintain that cadence despite changing conditions.

As with a car or motorbike, use a low gear to start off, so that you can build up speed easily. As momentum increases and pedalling becomes easier, change up to a higher gear.

When you climb a hill or face a headwind, change down until you can once more pedal at your optimum cadence. Approaching a hill, change down in good time so that you do not lose momentum unnecessarily.

Detect the point at which you need to pedal harder to maintain cadence and change down then.

CHANGING GEARS

Most cycle gears are of the derailleur type, which require continuous pedalling for gear changes.

This means that you must anticipate when you will need to stop so that you can change down in advance, in order to make restarting easier. If you need to stop at short notice, such as when a car overtakes and then stops in front without warning, pedal with the brakes applied, if necessary, in order to stop and change gear.

If your bike has hub gears, you do not need to pedal to change gear so you can change down after you have stopped. With hub gears, try rotating the pedals backwards a little after moving the gear lever to achieve an easier, smoother gear change.

If you have two gear mechanisms, the rear is used for small changes in gear ratios and the front for large changes. When you run out of gears at the back, change at the front and then modify the rear gear as necessary.

In steadily altering conditions, you can change up

or down one gear at a time. But if you turn a corner and the road goes up sharply, you will save time and momentum by changing through several gears in one go. This is when the front gear-changer can be very useful.

Gear changes should always be carried out smoothly and, when completed, the chain should not rub. Well executed gear changes are quiet.

Modern gear mechanisms change accurately as long as they are correctly adjusted.

RIDER CHECKLIST
- All gear changes should be smooth, precise and well-timed.
- Change down before stopping. This enables easier restarts.
- When cycling up hills, change down to maintain your cadence before you lose momentum.
- Consider multiple down-changes if you hit a sudden gradient.

3 // RIDING TECHNIQUES IN ACTION

Road basics

If you master all the fundamental riding techniques to the point where they become second nature, you'll have time left to hone your advanced cycling skills. This chapter explains how to achieve this worthwhile goal

JUNCTIONS

The majority of bike collisions involving another vehicle occur near 'T' junctions, crossroads, side turnings or roundabouts.

Almost all of these 'accidents' are caused by driver or rider error. According to statistics, the majority are not the fault of the cyclist, they are more likely to be sorry-mate-I-didn't-see-you situations, but it's the cyclist who almost always comes off worse.

By developing a systematic approach to your riding (ISPGA, page 26), you will massively reduce the likelihood of such an 'accident' happening to you.

Remember, in the following example ISPGA situations, each stage should be considered and used only where appropriate, not slavishly applied.

Aim to be a thinking rider, not an automaton.

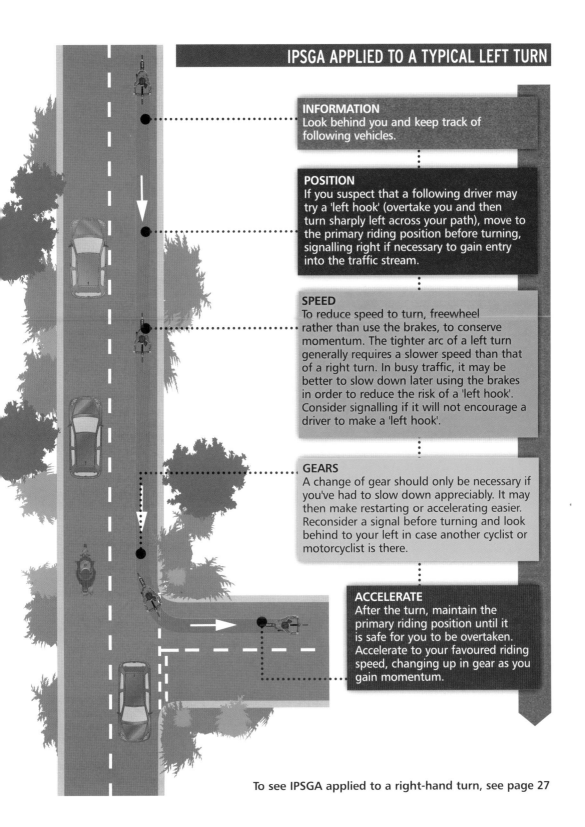

IPSGA APPLIED TO A TYPICAL LEFT TURN

INFORMATION
Look behind you and keep track of
following vehicles.

POSITION
If you suspect that a following driver may
try a 'left hook' (overtake you and then
turn sharply left across your path), move to
the primary riding position before turning,
signalling right if necessary to gain entry
into the traffic stream.

SPEED
To reduce speed to turn, freewheel
rather than use the brakes, to conserve
momentum. The tighter arc of a left turn
generally requires a slower speed than that
of a right turn. In busy traffic, it may be
better to slow down later using the brakes
in order to reduce the risk of a 'left hook'.
Consider signalling if it will not encourage a
driver to make a 'left hook'.

GEARS
A change of gear should only be necessary if
you've had to slow down appreciably. It may
then make restarting or accelerating easier.
Reconsider a signal before turning and look
behind to your left in case another cyclist or
motorcyclist is there.

ACCELERATE
After the turn, maintain the
primary riding position until it
is safe for you to be overtaken.
Accelerate to your favoured riding
speed, changing up in gear as you
gain momentum.

To see IPSGA applied to a right-hand turn, see page 27

51

IPSGA APPLIED TO TURNING RIGHT AT A ROUNDABOUT

INFORMATION
Look behind and scan the road ahead thoroughly to spot any hazards. Consider a signal to change course, one lane at a time.

POSITION
Approach the roundabout according to which exit you plan to take. If turning right, negotiate with drivers behind to move towards the centre of the road, one lane at a time. Adopt the primary position in each lane as you go.

SPEED
Accelerate, if necessary, to integrate with traffic. Then vary your speed to arrive at the give-way line when you can slot into traffic. If this is not possible, brake as you approach the give-way line.

GEAR
Change up in gear to help you accelerate across traffic, and then change gear to match your cadence as the manoeuvre develops. If you have to give-way, pedal as you brake to change down in gear and make restarting easier.

ACCELERATE
If you have kept going, accelerate once you cross the give-way line and move quickly through the roundabout. If you had to stop, you will need to wait for a greater gap in traffic to enter the traffic flow. Once on the roundabout, try not to stop, altering your speed using cadence, not your gears, so that you don't stall.

ACCELERATE
As you leave the roundabout, maintain the primary riding position until it is safe for you to be overtaken. Accelerate to your riding speed, changing up in gear as you gain momentum.

POSITION
Adopt the primary riding position throughout the roundabout to deter overtaking. Follow the path of other traffic, making exactly the same manoeuvre if you can. Keep aware of traffic to either side and behind. Consider signalling left to move across traffic.

ROUNDABOUTS

Generally, the safest course for a cycle to take through a roundabout, in the absence of other road users, is the shortest route from entry to exit (while negotiating the roundabout in the correct direction).

However, for all the examples shown here, we'll assume the presence of other road users.

Correct positioning and signalling are crucial at roundabouts and at busy roundabouts negotiation (see page 58) is needed to integrate with traffic and to encourage another road user to shield you. Assess the traffic flow on and near the roundabout continuously as you approach. Try to time your arrival to coincide with a gap in traffic so that you don't have to stop.

On the approach to a roundabout, change gear as necessary to match the speed at which you need to ride and to permit easy restarting if you have to slow down or stop. When you're on the roundabout, however, it is better to alter your cadence, not gears, to change speed, so that you do not stall at a point that could put you at risk from following vehicles.

Always be vigilant and never assume that other drivers will do as their signalling suggests.

Ride prominently at roundabouts, and keep aware of what's happening all around

MINI-ROUNDABOUTS

Right turns at mini-roundabouts can be tricky, as an approaching driver may not give way. Time your arrival when there is no traffic, or signal to an oncomer to let them go first.

Approach mini-roundabouts in the primary position, consider signalling, but keep both hands on the handlebar to turn. Avoid the central white dome as it can be slippery and cambered, but, if other drivers cross it, consider following to hold your position in the traffic.

Cyclists often negotiate confusing clusters of mini-roundabouts more easily than drivers.

Pay particular attention to approaching traffic at mini-roundabouts

SIGNALLING AT ROUNDABOUTS

On standard roundabouts, in the presence of other traffic, follow the advice in the *Highway Code*, but be aware of road markings that indicate special arrangements.

Below, you can see some suggested methods for dealing with a complicated six-exit roundabout.

TURNING LEFT (EXIT 1 OR 2)

Hold the primary position in the left-hand lane and consider signalling left on your approach (only if you're going to exit 1 and it does not encourage a following driver to try a 'left hook').

If you're taking exit 2, signal left as you pass the preceding entry, and keep your distance from traffic entering the roundabout.

STRAIGHT OVER (EXIT 3)

Approach in the centre of the left lane, holding the primary position.

Don't signal until you pass the preceding exit, then take care not to 'entice' following drivers to try a 'left hook'. Keep your distance from traffic at give-way lines.

In congested traffic, consider using the centre lane, holding the primary riding position until you pass the previous exit. Then signal left and spiral out towards your exit.

TURNING RIGHT (EXIT 4 OR 5)

Signal right, take the right-hand lane in the primary position and hold that position until past the exit preceding yours. Now, signal left (watching traffic on the left-hand side) and spiral out to your exit.

On three-lane roundabouts, think about using the centre lane for exit four. Change lanes one at a time, clearly and assertively with prominent road positioning.

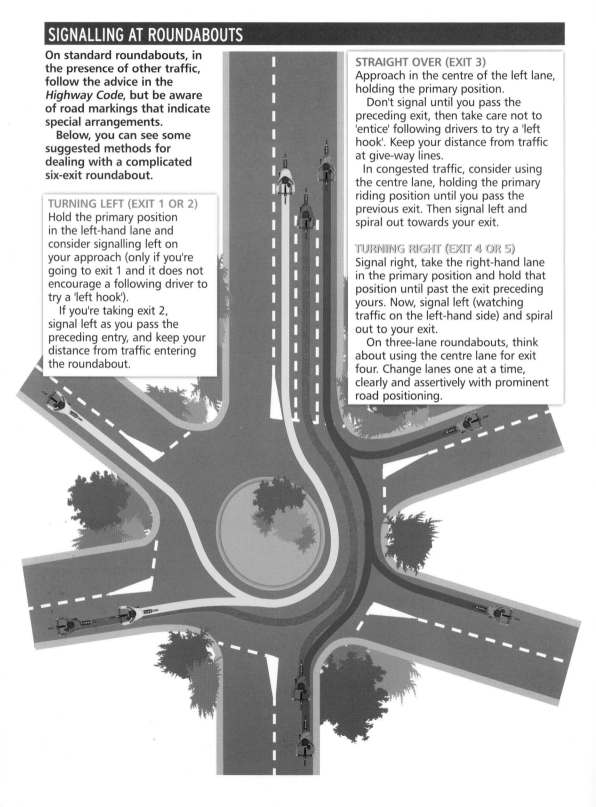

TURNING RIGHT AT CROSSROADS (OFF THE MAJOR ROUTE)

Position prominently whenever you turn right, making sure that other drivers have seen you. Engage eye contact if you can and occupy the primary riding position throughout the turn, unless you can gain protection from another vehicle turning right by positioning to its left side. Allow for the wide turning-path of long vehicles.

If an oncoming driver is also turning right, aim to pass right side-to-right side unless road markings dictate otherwise.

Always watch for people who behave differently and cooperate as best you can.

CROSSROADS AND 'T' JUNCTIONS

At junctions where you are on the minor route, or where neither route has precedence:
- Absorb information about junction layout and plan your approach early.
- Position according to the way you intend to go and in order to deter others from putting you at risk. Occupy a lane as you approach the give-way line.
- If you have to stop, change down gears on your approach so that you can restart quickly.
- When turning, check that the space you are turning into is clear. Be aware of cyclists and motorcyclists coming up from behind and filling the space.
- Signal if you have to cross traffic. Consider signals each time you change position, if it doesn't increase your risk.

- Make sure you are aware of the intentions of other drivers before pulling out. Don't rely on their direction indicators.
- Always be patient. In heavy traffic, don't take risks by entering too small a gap. Never cause other drivers to brake or swerve by your actions.
- Scan the surface as you manoeuvre, positioning early to avoid hazards.

If riding on a main road:
- Take your right of way if you can, but always allow yourself escape room if someone else acts unsafely towards you.
- Pay attention to other road users and always expect the worst from them, such as unsignalled manoeuvres, late braking and indecisiveness.
- When approaching a junction where another vehicle is waiting to turn, try to engage eye contact with the driver if you can, but don't assume you've been seen because they are looking towards you. Consider adjusting your position on the road to make yourself more prominent and to allow 'escape room' if they pull out in front of you. If you are not sure if you have been seen, reduce your speed and be ready to brake.
- Always aim to be considerate, but at the same time never put courtesy ahead of practicality or safety. For example, only let someone into the traffic before you if you can regain momentum easily and it won't cause undue braking by drivers behind you.

Always stop in the centre of a lane at traffic signals

Good planning on approach to traffic lights can make your progress through a junction easier and safer.

Look ahead and position according to the direction you intend to go. Always adopt the primary riding position in the appropriate lane.

Try to adjust your speed to arrive at the lights when they are green. If this requires you to slow down, watch out for other drivers trying to make unsafe overtaking manoeuvres.

If you are first in the queue at traffic lights, pull up a short distance before the stop line. You can use the space in front to gain balance as the lights change from red, without crossing the line before the green light shows. However, don't set-off early like this if there are pedestrians about.

Never pull-up too close behind other traffic at lights. Hold the lane, but move side-ways just enough to be visible in a mirror of the vehicle stopped in front.

If you can't see the lights for the other routes, look for signs of the traffic slowing as their signals go red. Use this anticipation to your advantage but don't cross the line until your lights change to green.

Only use a cycle lane leading up to an advanced stop line, if it is to your advantage. Keep in the main traffic lane if the lights are likely to be green upon your arrival or if the cycle lane is narrow. It is not uncommon for passengers to open car doors while waiting at lights. If you do filter past traffic to an advanced stop line, aim to adopt the primary riding position and remain visable, but never use a kerb-side cycle lane to access an advanced stop line when turning right. To turn right at lights, position yourself in the same way as other traffic.

RIDER CHECKLIST
- Remember, all junctions are hazards.
- Always consider signalling well in advance of a manoeuvre and take up the correct road position decisively.
- Pull away from a junction only when it's completely safe to do so.
- Always select the correct lane and signalling procedure when approaching and negotiating roundabouts. Your entry and exit should be decisive, well-observed and safe. Prominent positioning is essential.
- Use cycle lanes and other facilities at junctions only if it is to your advantage. Be aware that many cycle facilities complicate the traffic situation and can increase risk.

Negotiation

A bicycle is small and lacks the power of other vehicles on the road. But that doesn't mean you can't take your place in traffic and carry out complex manoeuvres safely. Negotiation is the technique by which you get other road users to cooperate and protect you as you ride

ESTABLISHING NEGOTIATION

Negotiation is all about cooperation. It makes other drivers want to assist you by appealing to a basic human instinct – responding with help when it is specifically requested. You seek to influence the positive actions of others to your best cycling advantage.
The basic stages of a cycling negotiation are:
● Keep track of vehicles following you.
● Choose a driver with whom to negotiate. Good choices are drivers who keep more road space in front of them, which suggests less haste and

a more careful approach to their driving. Unless traffic speeds are low, you shouldn't normally seek to intercept a large vehicle, bus or another two-wheeler, who may have more difficulty responding.
● With a small movement towards traffic, or signalling, or both, make a 'please-let-me-in' request to the following driver.
● If the driver responds by slowing down or leaving you additional space, move quickly into the traffic stream in front of the cooperating driver.
If you need to cross several lanes of traffic, as when turning right off a multi-lane road,

you carry out this procedure lane-by-lane, holding each lane in the primary riding position, under the protection of the driver behind, until you can enter the next lane.
Although most drivers respond quickly to a well-executed negotiation request, you need to allow for those who do not. The whole procedure can take some distance to complete, depending upon traffic speed. To allow time for this, so that you can start negotiating early, keep aware of conditions ahead of you from the middle to the far distance.

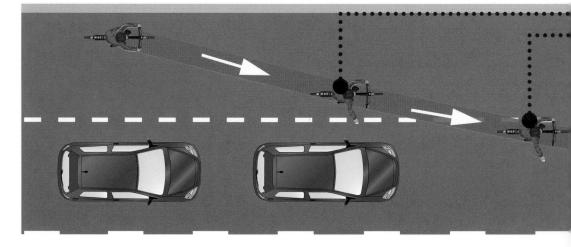

The cyclist makes eye-contact with the following driver to negotiate a move across lanes

OVERTAKING BY NEGOTIATION

1) MOVE ACROSS THE NEARSIDE LANE

Move to the primary riding position in the lane that is obstructed and then towards its right side. This should not be difficult as vehicles behind you will also be changing lanes.

Check traffic behind and, as a suitable gap arrives, signal right to indicate that you want to enter the traffic stream.

2) WAIT FOR A COOPERATION RESPONSE

At the start of the gap, move on to the white lane line, reinforcing the fact that you want to intercept traffic. Consider whether to continue signalling. If the next driver lets you in, move quickly into the traffic flow. If he doesn't, move a little left and repeat the sequence with another driver.

3)STAY IN TRAFFIC UNTIL IT IS SAFE TO LEAVE

Ride well clear of the vehicles you pass to allow for a door opening or someone walking out.

If you are overtaking more than one vehicle at a time, hold the primary riding position throughout the entire manoeuvre.

Move back to the left-hand side only when it is safe for you to be passed.

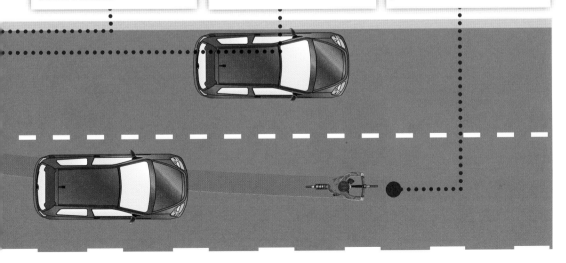

TURNING RIGHT BY NEGOTIATION (READ FROM THE BOTTOM OF THE PAGE)

3) PROTECT YOURSELF BEFORE TURNING

Direct your attention ahead to select a gap in oncoming traffic where you can turn right safely.

Don't get too close to the centre line and if you need to wait, adopt a position that will deter other turning drivers from passing you.

If vehicles ahead are turning, follow them, positioning so that their drivers can see you and you can see oncoming traffic.

2) NEGOTIATE INTO THE SECOND LANE

Keep track of traffic in the second lane. It may be moving faster than traffic in the nearside lane so select a longer gap to allow for this.

Move to the right side of the nearside lane and signal right. Do not leave the first lane until a driver in the next lane has allowed you to continue. When that happens, move quickly to the primary riding position in that lane.

Repeat this process if you need to cross more lanes in your direction.

1) NEGOTIATE INTO THE NEARSIDE LANE

Keep track of traffic behind and choose a suitable gap. Signal right and move a little in that direction to issue a negotiation request.

Decide whether the next driver will let you in. If so, move to the primary riding position and hold the lane.

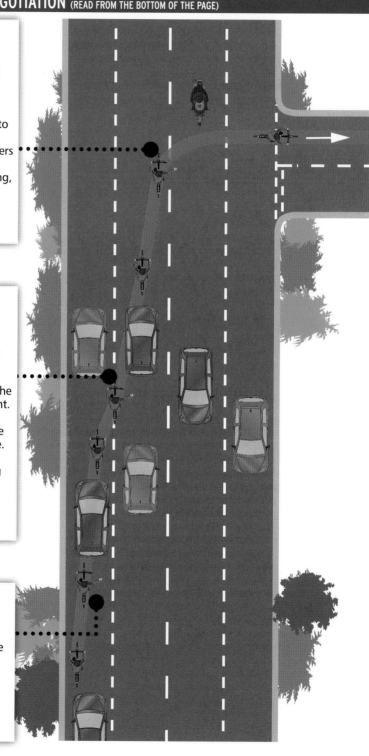

How to be a better cyclist

NEGOTIATION AT ROUNDABOUTS

Cyclists are vulnerable on busy roundabouts as they are not always easily seen by other drivers who have many things to concentrate on. Negotiation is a key skill for using roundabouts safely, by persuading other drivers to shield you as you execute the manoeuvre

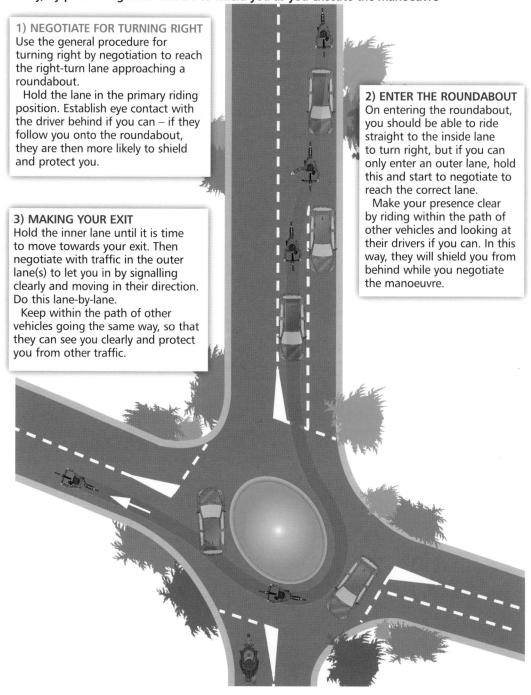

1) NEGOTIATE FOR TURNING RIGHT
Use the general procedure for turning right by negotiation to reach the right-turn lane approaching a roundabout.

Hold the lane in the primary riding position. Establish eye contact with the driver behind if you can – if they follow you onto the roundabout, they are then more likely to shield and protect you.

2) ENTER THE ROUNDABOUT
On entering the roundabout, you should be able to ride straight to the inside lane to turn right, but if you can only enter an outer lane, hold this and start to negotiate to reach the correct lane.

Make your presence clear by riding within the path of other vehicles and looking at their drivers if you can. In this way, they will shield you from behind while you negotiate the manoeuvre.

3) MAKING YOUR EXIT
Hold the inner lane until it is time to move towards your exit. Then negotiate with traffic in the outer lane(s) to let you in by signalling clearly and moving in their direction. Do this lane-by-lane.

Keep within the path of other vehicles going the same way, so that they can see you clearly and protect you from other traffic.

RIDER CHECKLIST
- Know what's behind you before you start to negotiate a manoeuvre.
- Break down a complex manoeuvre into a series of simpler parts. Complete each part of the manoeuvre one by one.
- Hold your current space on the road until it is safe to move on.
- Thank people who cooperate with a wave or a smile.

Cycling in town

Cycling in towns and cities is arguably the most demanding. Enhanced concentration and observation are essential, but the pay-back for cyclists is huge, both in terms of freedom of movement and speed of progress

THE EXTRA DEMANDS OF TOWN CYCLING

Denser traffic and lots of pedestrians in towns and cities result in a concentration of problems for cyclists, with hazards appearing frequently.

Hazards are also more likely to be concealed, and there are more junctions and traffic lights to deal with.

The only way to cope safely with all these potential dangers is to observe and concentrate intensely, spotting the hazards early and making the appropriate preparations as soon as possible.

Local knowledge is useful in town, but should never lure you into a false sense of security, as most crashes occur near home, where road-users can be most complacent.

Good positioning is essential in towns, so that you can clearly see and be seen. You will often be able to use the primary riding position as your speed will be comparable with that of other traffic.

Getting into the correct lane at junctions is important. To do this, you'll need to look ahead at the way traffic is moving.

ROUTE OBSERVATION IN TOWN

Good observation in town helps you spot many hazards and identify useful information to assist your cycling. Here are some important things to look out for:

● Parked cars can obscure hazards. As you pass them, choose a speed and road position that gives you enough reaction time if, for example, a door is opened without warning or someone steps out.

● Spot tell-tale signs that a vehicle is about to pull out: angled wheels, exhaust smoke and illuminated tail-lights etc.

● Look out for pedestrians crossing the road. At crossings, many people start to walk when the green man 'beeps' without looking if any traffic is approaching. Also look out for 'late runners', who make a dash for it as your lights turn green.

● Be aware of pedestrians near schools and pubs at key times, and near offices and stations etc at all times.

● Beware of other cyclists and motorcyclists who may filter from behind.

Cars, buses and traffic signals. There's a lot to observe at a busy junction

● Watch buses and other tall vehicles up ahead. They can give an early warning as to traffic movements.

● Lorries and buses can obscure important road signs. Looking ahead for signs will minimise this problem.

● Delivery vans often park in awkward places, so take extra care when passing them.

Look underneath them to spot the feet of pedestrians who may step out into the road without warning.

● Taxis may make unexpected manoeuvres (U-turns, sudden stops) when they spot a fare. Be especially prepared for this when cycling near places like railway and coach stations and shopping centres.

FILTERING

An important advantage of cycling is the ability to filter through congested traffic, which is one reason why cyclists can often travel more quickly in towns than other road users. However, advantages in saving time must be balanced against your increased vulnerability while filtering. Also, some road-users believe that filtering through traffic is illegal (it isn't) and can react to it in a hostile or obstructive manner.

Key points to bear in mind when filtering are:

● Where possible, filter to the right of traffic, but if that

means riding close to the centre of the road ensure that there is enough space between you and oncoming traffic.

Do not cross the centre white line if it is continuous or if there are vehicles approaching.

● Don't get stuck in tight spaces that could close-in on you. Only filter where there is room to spare, so that you have plenty of warning if anyone moves towards you.

● Don't filter in traffic that is moving faster than about six to eight mph. You should always have sufficient speed in reserve to outpace a vehicle that you are overtaking.

● Keep alert for pedestrians crossing and vehicle doors opening unexpectedly.

● Obey the normal *Highway Code* rules at traffic signals and pedestrian crossings.

Do not filter past a stop line (or a cyclist's advanced stop line, where present) when the signal is still at red.

● *Never pass alongside a long vehicle or bus unless there is plenty of space, and you're certain you can get past before it moves off. Filtering to the left of long (or heavy) vehicles near junctions is a common cause of fatalities. (See page 68)*

Slow-moving rush hour traffic is easy to pass for the advanced cyclist

OBSERVATION AND 'STEPPING STONES'

As well as observing the near and middle-distance when filtering, the advanced cyclist makes use of peripheral vision. This is an effective way of spotting changes in the traffic all around you.

Look well ahead to plan your route and use your peripheral vision to monitor traffic on either side of you. If you sense something moving unexpectedly, scan around to check it out. Once satisfied, return to the distance vision and repeat.

Avoid target fixation – when your vision fixates on one particular thing, such as a vehicle in the foreground – as any escape route becomes invisible to you. Advanced cyclists observe, scan, identify, predict, prioritise and act.

In queues of traffic, use distance vision to identify safe 'refuge points', that you can move to one at a time, just like stepping stones in a stream. These are places where there are larger gaps in traffic that will accommodate you

and protect you from moving traffic, without inconveniencing another driver.

Always endeavour to filter from one 'stepping stone' to another. However, be aware that any gaps could be filled by someone else without warning.

If a driver sees a fleeting opportunity to move into a faster lane, don't assume they will be checking their mirror before they do so. Always have a 'Plan B' to put into action should such a dangerous eventuality occur.

POINTS TO REMEMBER WHEN FILTERING

When filtering past traffic, think about the following questions:

- Do you have an escape route planned at all times?
- Have you allowed yourself sufficient distance from other traffic (and pedestrians) to allow you time to react?
- When passing a high-sided vehicle, could a pedestrian step out from behind it?
- Where vehicles start moving off, but one remains stationary, is it letting someone or something out?
- When a driver is left space to emerge from a side turning and turn right (see below), will he be concentrating to the left as the bonnet of his car extends beyond the line of traffic? Is he likely to spot a filtering cyclist?
- Look into vehicle mirrors. Can you see the driver's eyes? Are they looking at you? If not, they probably cannot see you at all and will not know that you are even there.
- If you don't need to be close to the vehicles you are filtering past, move well clear.

You're easier to see if you are separated from them and you have more room for manoeuvre if one of them changes direction without warning.

- When approaching traffic lights at red or changing to red, do not filter past the first vehicle in a queue unless there is an advanced stop line and you are confident that you can reach it before the next green light. Always endeavour to adopt the primary riding position behind the first driver, or further back, and let those in front concentrate on choosing a safe moment to move off.
- Do not ride at a speed far in excess of the traffic flow, as this will limit your time to react if anything unexpected happens.

At first glance, this looks like a good opportunity to filter...

... but the advanced cyclist will have noticed the gap in the queue and the break in the chevrons, and anticipated the unsighted car emerging

UNDERTAKING

This is one of the most dangerous manoeuvres in cycling. Never cycle up the inside of a long or heavy vehicle that's turning left

Filtering between the kerb and stationary traffic is sometimes referred to as undertaking – with good reason! This is always a hazardous place to ride and no safer if there is a cycle lane marked. Drivers or their passengers in a jam often open their doors unexpectedly.

Passengers are the most likely to make an error, as they cannot make use of rear-view mirrors which are angled for the driver to use, and few will ask the driver if it is safe to open the door.

If you look closely at a car door, the top edge has the appearance of a blade – not something that you want to be hitting at any speed!

Along the kerbside, you will also be more likely to encounter drain covers, surface erosion, general litter and debris and, possibly, wet road markings – all are hazardous.

A hallmark of an advanced cyclist is to keep away from the kerb zone as much as possible.

ROAD SURFACES IN TOWN

Road surfaces change frequently in town. You will often have to deal with potholes, poorly reinstated trenches and protruding manhole covers, as well as engineering features such as speed humps and tables and blockwork surfacing. All of these are potential hazards for a cyclist and all the more so when traffic is heavy or surfaces wet.

By constantly scanning the road surface ahead for as far as you can see, you can get warning of problems. Poor surfaces can often be distinguished by a change of colour or texture. Expect these to be a hazard, unless it is proved otherwise.

Having identified a potential hazard, you must quickly react to it. If possible, change your position on the road to avoid the defect, taking care to signal and/or negotiate with drivers as necessary. If you're not going to be able to avoid a defect, prepare to cross it

White lines can be very slippery when wet

New potholes can appear quickly after snow and ice

Potholes can damage your cycle and cause you to lose control

Avoid deep puddles, for obvious reasons

squarely with the handlebar straight and lift your weight off the saddle. With a ridge to cross, you should reduce speed. If there's a depression in the

surface, you may be better off accelerating so that your bike can 'fly' across. You need to judge what's best according to the circumstances.

Cracks and ridges in your direction of travel can throw a bike. Ride clear

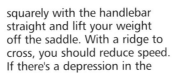

BUS LANES

Cyclists are allowed to use most bus lanes. You should ride in the centre of the lane unless you need to be overtaken by another authorised user and there is sufficient space for this to take place safely.

Bus lanes are usually safer than cycle lanes as they are wider, but make sure that you are seen by traffic entering and leaving side roads, which may cut across your path without warning. Sometimes motorcycles are allowed to use bus lanes and their position in the lane will be similar to where cyclists should ride. If they start to overtake to your right, give them space to do so, but watch out for the motorcyclist or another cyclist who attempts to undertake to your left, especially at the approach to a turning.

If a bus stops ahead of you in a bus lane and there is insufficient room in the lane to pass, overtake by moving to the next lane if it is safe to do so. Otherwise hold back (reduce speed as you approach) until the bus moves off.

CONFIDENCE IN CONGESTED CONDITIONS

City cyclists, used to congested streets, generally appear more assertive than those who ride predominantly on quieter roads. A city rider may seem pushy, as they make confident progress, but their style is in response to their congested surroundings. It helps to avoid hold-ups and this more decisive approach to cycling is less physically demanding than staying in stop-go traffic.

As long as city cyclists know what they are doing, where they are going and are considerate to others, including pedestrians, their decisive manner won't cause problems.

Adapt your riding to suit the situation around you. Be as decisive and assertive as conditions require by carefully positioning your machine on the road. Strive to make good progress while giving yourself room to manoeuvre.

RIDER CHECKLIST
● **Riding in town requires highly-developed, selective observation skills to process all the information you'll have to take in.**
● **When you stop in traffic, don't pull up too close to a vehicle in front, and ensure you can be seen by the driver in a mirror.**
● **Practise your manoeuvring skills until they become instinctive, so that you are free to concentrate on the traffic situation around you.**
● **The advanced cyclist requires good anticipation to spot unexpected movements by pedestrians, parked vehicles, motorcyclists and other cyclists.**
● **Filter with extreme care. Do not pass too close to long vehicles (lorries, vans and buses) that could turn across your path.**

Cycle facilities

Advanced cyclists often choose to stay on the road with traffic, rather than use a cycle path. Here's why...

In the UK, there is no legal obligation for cyclists to use any kind of cycle facility. They are there to use if you wish, as an alternative to riding with general traffic, not as a mandatory substitute.

According to statistics, a lot of existing cycle facilities have little if any safety benefit.

Some introduce significant new hazards and lead to unsafe cycling practices. The advanced cyclist should consider facilities more from the point of view of convenience than safety. You may find them useful where they give you a shorter, quicker or more pleasant journey.

Always be discriminating and cautious, having regard to local circumstances. Ride within the limits of what you can see to be safe and your capabilities, never on the assumption that a route is safer just because it is marked for use by cyclists.

Take advantage of facilities where they help you, but ignore those that don't.

CYCLE LANES

Roads with cycle lanes are multi-lane roads. Most drivers use their lane without too much concern about what's happening in the next lane – as they can drive straight past adjacent traffic, they do not need to think about overtaking it. As a result, motorists often pass cyclists closer and faster where there is a cycle lane than where there isn't, especially where lanes are narrower than the recommended width of two metres.

Although drivers do not need to change lanes to pass a cyclist who is in a cycle lane, a cyclist does need to change lanes when negotiating obstacles such as parked cars. In this instance, the rules of negotiation apply (see 'Negotiation' on page 58). This reverses the principle of priority on ordinary roads and can be confusing and less safe for everyone involved.

Using a cycle lane to bypass queuing traffic is just a form of filtering next to the kerb, which is the most dangerous place to filter.

It is almost impossible to avoid an opening car door in most cycle lanes.

At junctions, you also become vulnerable to traffic turning left across your cycle lane.

Passing side roads, cycle lanes direct you into the very place where risk is greatest, close to the give-way road markings.

Try not to let the presence of a cycle lane affect your decision as to where it is safest to ride. Position yourself as if the lane is not there, but be extra careful when moving out of a lane, as other road users may not expect you to do so.

Cycle lanes this narrow can greatly increase risk

Treat the movement like that of changing lanes on a multi-lane road, moving right by negotiation well in advance of where you need to be in the new position.

CYCLE PATHS NEXT TO THE ROAD

Every junction along a cycle track is a high-risk location. Take great care how you proceed

These may be purpose-built cycle tracks or redesignated footways for shared-use by cyclists and pedestrians.

These paths increase danger at every road and driveway crossing, as cyclists using them need to look through a much wider arc for potential conflict (see below) and road users have to look more widely than usual to see cyclists.

When collisions occur, they tend to be more serious than most collisions on the road. Moreover, cycle path users usually have to give way to road users at every crossing or, if they have priority, there is a high risk of it not being respected by the motorist.

Advanced cyclists usually have little use for roadside paths. About the only time they might be useful, is if the adjacent road is heavily congested and there is a long distance between junctions. In these circumstances, expect to ride more slowly and submissively and to exercise much more vigilance and tolerance than would be the case on the road. You cannot depend upon anyone else being concerned with your safety.

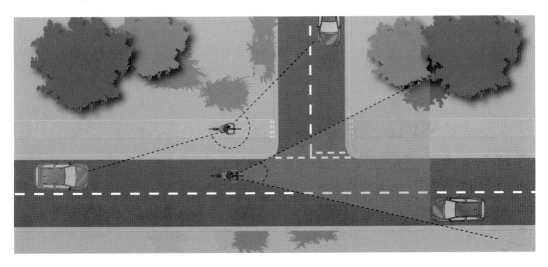

How to be a better cyclist

REACTIONS OF OTHER DRIVERS

Many drivers think that cyclists should use cycle lanes and tracks where they are provided. They do not understand the difficulties that cycle facilities can introduce and may be hostile to cyclists who do not choose to use them.

Handle these situations as best you can, continuing to ride where you consider to be safest and most convenient, if possible. If compromising between riding where it is safest and riding where it incurs the least wrath from others, be aware of the consequences of doing so and adjust your riding accordingly. It may be better to find a different route next time.

> "Always expect others not to have seen you and have a diversionary strategy in mind"

OTHER CYCLE FACILITIES

Legal exemptions for cyclists, including banned turns, road closures and other controls on traffic are generally the most useful of all facilities, and can permit quicker and more direct journeys. Contra-flow cycle lanes may also save a considerable detour, though you may find yourself cycling closer to oncoming traffic than on a two-way road.

With all these facilities, make allowance for pedestrians and drivers who might not expect the movement you are making. Always expect others not to have seen you and have a diversionary strategy in mind in case you find yourself on a collision course.

Off-road cycle trails, such as those along old railway lines, sometimes afford pleasant and useful routes, but only occasionally are they speedy ones. These, too, are not inherently safe routes – no safer than most roads. User discipline can be a particular problem. To benefit from these trails, you need to recognise their limitations, and expect others not to do likewise.

RIDER CHECKLIST

- Weigh up carefully the pros and cons of cycle facilities you encounter. Do not use them just because they are there.
- Expect to have greater responsibility for your safety when riding away from traffic.
- Always allow for other people not expecting you to ride where you do.

Cycling in the countryside

Cycling is one of the best ways to enjoy our amazing countryside. Cyclists enjoy the peace and serenity of the countryside, as they make so little impact on it

MAIN ROADS

These are the fast, main arteries where most of the traffic is, and it's usually going fast.

If you want to get quickly from town to town, you may need to use these roads for much of your journey. Even when trying to avoid main roads, you might have to cross

them or ride along them at some point in your journey. The secondary position is where you should normally ride on these roads. When you need to cross traffic, or emphasise your presence because of a hazard ahead, allow extra time for manoeuvring to take account

of traffic speed. Negotiation can be used when speeds are moderate, but, when traffic is moving close to the national speed limit, it is preferable to use extended gaps in traffic, slowing or stopping if necessary until an opportunity to manoeuvre arises.

COUNTRY LANES

Country lanes often provide ideal cycling conditions. Not all lanes are idyllic; some are used as rat-runs and elsewhere motorists sometimes drive much faster than is safe on roads that are narrow or which twist and turn. So while you can usually relax more when cycling on country lanes, you still need to stay alert to other people acting unsafely.

In the quiet of the countryside, your ears can give you early warning of a vehicle approaching and of how it is being driven.

Where there is little traffic, the preferred place to ride in the country is in the primary riding position. This means that you will most easily be seen when another vehicle does come along and bike control

will be easiest. In practice, on single-track lanes, debris in the centre of the road may not permit a central riding position and you should ride to the left or right according to the suitability of the surface and to maximise forward visibility.

On bends, position yourself for the best view ahead. This also gives oncoming drivers the earliest view of you.

CLIMBING HILLS

Cycling up long inclines or steep hills requires expert use of your gears, proper technique and patience.

You should start to change down in gear before you have to reduce your cadence. You do this by detecting the increase in pedalling effort that precedes a reduction in pedalling speed. The aim is to maintain the same cadence until you reach the point where you can change down in gear no more.

You will waste much less momentum on steep hills by changing down several gears at a time, such as by moving to the smallest front chainwheel. After reaching bottom gear, your cadence will decrease, but it will usually still be easier to pedal than to walk. Lean forward to stop the front wheel lifting and zig-zag up the hill if the way ahead is clear.

Where the road zigzags, follow a line around the outside of the bends if you can, as the gradient should be less severe.

If there is traffic around, be cautious about trying too hard to ride in a straight line. If other road users sense that bike control is easier for you than is actually the case, they may fail to give you as much consideration and clearance when passing as you need.

DESCENDING HILLS

Descending hills can be exhilarating, but requires a great deal of concentration and control, as conditions around you change quickly and the consequences of a fall at high-speed could be serious.

At the start of every descent, check that your brakes are working. Then keep them applied, so that you never reach a speed so fast that you can't stop within the distance that you can see to be clear.

On single-track roads you must be able to stop in half the distance you can see to be clear.

On long, steep hills, 'pumping' the brakes on and off can help reduce heat and brake fade. Where there is no traffic, zig-zagging downwards (like a skier traversing a slope), can reduce the mean gradient.

Change up gears as you ride faster, so that you can easily resume pedalling if you need to avoid a hazard.

THE 'LIMIT POINT OF VISION'

When you are riding fast down a hill where the road curves sharply, you need to take care that you can negotiate bends without ending up in a verge or riding into oncoming traffic.

The 'Limit Point' is the furthest point ahead where you have a clear view of the road surface. This determines how fast you can safely enter a bend. The closer the 'Limit Point', the less time and distance you have in which to act and therefore the slower you need to go.

Watch the 'Limit Point' as you approach a bend and you'll notice that it may move. If it becomes closer than the distance in which you can stop, slow down. If the 'Limit Point' continues to get closer, the bend is tightening and you will need to slow down more. On the other hand, when the 'Limit Point' starts to move away, you can safely regain speed.

Moving right can improve your vision around a left-hand bend

CATTLE GRIDS AND FORDS

Cattle grids differ greatly in their impact on a cycle. Some are very uncomfortable and, where bars are missing or damaged, can be dangerous. The faster you cross, the less discomfort you will feel, but if a grid is unsafe you will have less time to take evasive action. As you approach, decide whether to accelerate or slow down. Hold the handlebar firmly and freewheel as you cross the grid at a right-angle to the bars. In the wet, metal surfaces like cattle grids and railway lines can be slippery.

Fords can be hazardous if too deep, fast-flowing or slippery, but otherwise are often enjoyed by cyclists! Always inspect a ford before crossing, then select a low gear, ride straight and pedal all the time.

HORSES

Take care when you meet horses on a country road, as they are easily frightened by a moving bicycle. Attract the rider's attention and wait for permission to pass. Exchange a few words of greeting as this can reassure the horse.

Pass the horse and rider slowly, giving them plenty of room, if possible by crossing to the opposite side of the road.

RIDER CHECKLIST
- Stay alert for traffic travelling fast on country roads. Defer and wait for a safe gap to appear if necessary.
- Use your position on lanes to maximise forward visibility and to avoid poor road surfaces.
- Practise smooth gear changes to enable you to cycle up hills more easily. Be patient.
- Always keep your bike under control when descending hills. Use your brakes to maintain a safe speed and take extra care through bends.

Cycling in tricky conditions

Advanced cyclists are able to ride with skill and precision in all conditions, including difficult situations in the day or at night. These tips will help you achieve that goal

CYCLING AT NIGHT

The fundamental rule of a systematic approach to your cycling – that you must be able to stop within the distance you can see to be clear – is especially important when riding at night.

Away from street lighting, your vision will be limited to the range of your bike's front light, so you should fit the best you can afford. Aim the light at the road about 10 metres ahead, so that it lights your way and is clearly visible to oncoming drivers. Direct the light so that you can see the road edge clearly, or, where there is no traffic, follow the centre line.

Wherever you ride at night, it will be harder for others to see you and it will be harder for everyone to judge conditions. Be more cautious in traffic, allowing time for you to be seen and your intentions understood. Techniques such as negotiation are more difficult to carry out when visibility is poor and it is usually better to wait for a gap in traffic before crossing its path.

Surface defects are more difficult to spot and dodge at night where lighting is poor. Don't ride too fast, avoid the road edge and maintain firm control over your steering, always with both hands on the handlebar. 'Jumping over' potholes (pull up hard on the handlebar as you cross) can be a very useful last-second avoidance technique.

SOME ADVANTAGES OF CYCLING AT NIGHT

Riding in the dark isn't all about hazards and drawbacks. There are some advantages, and if there isn't much traffic around, it can be very enjoyable.

The lights of other vehicles give useful clues as to what might happen. It is easier to spot a car that is about to pull out of a line of parked vehicles. On country roads with little traffic, you get advance notice of someone coming from their lights. Light beams can also help you to work out where the road you're on goes next, as can street and house lighting.

Don't be complacent though, speed and distance are difficult to judge in the dark, especially the speed of approaching vehicles. Alter your own speed to arrive at potential conflict places after other drivers.

DAZZLE

One of the most serious hazards when cycling at night is the dazzle caused by oncoming drivers, who do not dip their vehicle lights as you approach. If blinded, you are likely to ride straight towards the source of the light.

When you meet a vehicle coming in the opposite direction on an unlit road, keep track of its progress without looking straight at it. Focus your attention on the road ahead, making sure that you stay a safe distance from the edge of the road. If you are dazzled, slow down, look just ahead of your front wheel and be prepared to stop.

Sometimes a flash of your front light by deflecting the handlebar – moving it briefly in one direction, then back in the other – can remind a driver to dip their lights.

CYCLING WHEN IT'S WINDY

Wind is the principal weather problem for cycling. It can make journeys tiring and can also add significantly to risk, if it makes control of your bicycle more difficult to maintain.

To battle against a headwind, get your body as low and as streamlined as you can. Change to a lower gear to maintain your usual cadence and try to steer as straight a course as possible. If you have dropped handlebars and there are no imminent traffic hazards, use the dropped position.

If you have to ride more slowly, you may not be able to integrate with traffic so easily. Wind also makes it more difficult to hear traffic. Take care not to drift too close to the road edge as accurate and consistent steering is more difficult in strong wind.

Crosswinds are the most hazardous and can move a bicycle – and sometimes larger

vehicles – significant sideways distances across a road. Keep your body down, use a low gear and take firm control of the steering. You will need to steer towards the wind to go straight ahead, but be alert for sudden changes to conditions

in blustery winds or in the lee of buildings and when you meet another vehicle.

When the wind is strong, you may find it less tiring and just as quick to use a more indirect route where there is shelter from hedges and/or less traffic.

RAIN

Rain (without strong wind) does not have to be unpleasant for cycling, if you wear waterproof clothing made of breathable fabrics.

The main problem is that your brakes will work less well – perhaps much less so. You must allow additional time for braking and be more cautious approaching potential hazards. Brake with equal force on front and rear brakes.

In heavy rain, it can take several seconds before your brakes begin to work as the blocks must first clear the rims of water. Continue to apply pressure gently; squeezing hard may cause a wheel to lock when contact is made. It's a good idea to chase water off the rims as you ride by applying the brakes lightly, so that you're better prepared if you need to stop.

Spray from overtaking traffic is a problem, even when it has stopped raining. Try to pace your riding so that you're not overtaken near large puddles. Watch out for puddles that are deep potholes in disguise.

If you wear spectacles, it's best to take them off in heavy rain, as long as you can still see well enough to cycle safely. Be aware that other drivers' visibility may also be impaired.

FOG AND MIST

Cyclists are very vulnerable when visibility is bad. Use high-visibility clothing as well as lights, as cycle lamps are much less effective in fog and mist.

In dense fog, ride closer to the road edge, instead of

holding the secondary riding position, as other drivers will find it much harder to see you. It also makes it easier to follow the road.

Ride more slowly, ready for surface hazards, and use your

ears to detect other vehicles. Consider shouting or ringing your bell if it might help someone to notice you.

Fog and mist can also impair braking. Take the precautions recommended for heavy rain.

RIDING WHEN IT'S COLD

Snow and ice make cycling more difficult, but by no means impossible, especially if you can keep away from busy roads. However, if you doubt your ability to cope, it's best not to travel if you don't have to.

- Wrap up well, especially head, hands and feet.
- Gloves or mittens should not impede use of the brake levers.
- Always assume there'll be ice on the road after a cold night and ride cautiously. Even if most roads are clear, there may still be ice hollows. Remember, black ice is very difficult to see.
- Reducing tyre pressure a little can give better adhesion on slippery surfaces.
- Make every manoeuvre gently, especially cornering and braking. Ride slowly, in a lower gear than usual, regulating speed by changing your cadence. Keep both hands on the handlebar.
- Don't make sharp turns or be rushed by traffic. Ride in a very considered way: stop, check that all is clear, change direction if necessary and ride off again. If looking behind or signalling are difficult, stop and use gaps to cross traffic.
- If you ride onto ice, you will probably not fall if you stay relaxed and hold a straight line.

Cycling in summer

Most cyclists hit the road in summer. Here are some tips on getting the most out of cycling in the sun...

In summer weather, cycling is the perfect way to travel. With a little preparation, you can make your cycle ride even more enjoyable and relaxing.

Take sunglasses and/or a peaked hat on a sunny summer ride, to protect your eyes, enhance your vision and keep bugs at bay.

Dehydration is possible if you cycle a long distance in hot weather, and sunburn may occur if your skin is not protected. It's important to drink regularly whenever you make long journeys, but especially so if it's hot.

Be aware that you or another road user may be temporarily blinded by the sun, especially when it's low in the sky. This can happen as easily in town as in the country. If you are riding towards or away from the direction of the sun, make extra allowance for the possibility that any driver heading towards it may be blinded and might not see you.

If you're blinded, focus on the road just ahead and slow down as necessary.

There are few past-times more healthy and enjoyable than cycling on a beautiful summer's day

Low sunlight can seriously restrict your vision and that of other drivers. Focus on the road in front to avoid being blinded

RIDER CHECKLIST
- Be aware that it's more difficult to judge distance and speed in the dark.
- Ensure that you can always stop safely within the distance that you can see to be clear in your cycle lamp illumination.
- Keep your lights clean and replace the batteries when the light output decreases. Consider carrying spare batteries with you.
- Stop for a rest from time to time. Tiredness affects reaction times and concentration.
- Always consider the weather conditions when setting out on a cycle ride. If they are very bad, postpone your journey.
- Modify your behaviour if the weather is bad in order to minimise risk. This may mean being less assertive in your riding and pausing from time to time until it is safe to proceed.
- Allow for the impact of weather conditions on another driver's ability to see you.

Roadworks

Diversions and roadworks are a fact of life on Britain's roads. Here's how to respond to them to minimise disruptions to your journey

ROADWORKS

Treat minor roadworks the same as any other obstruction, using the normal techniques for overtaking to pass. Look out for the road surface being uneven or muddy.

More significant works are where one side of the road may be closed for some distance, with all traffic being routed – first in one direction, then the other – on the other side. The usable space is often too narrow for a cycle to be passed safely by another vehicle and the state of the road surface may add to the danger. In these situations, adopt the primary riding position to deter anyone from overtaking, but do pass along as quickly as you can.

It is not a good idea to let following traffic go first as you are then more likely to be confronted with traffic in the other direction before you can clear the restriction.

Cyclists have the option of dismounting and pushing their bike to avoid long roadwork delays

DIVERSIONS

When a road is closed entirely, the diversionary route may be significantly longer from a cyclist's point of view (sometimes several miles longer) and may involve the use of less pleasant roads.

In most cases, cyclists can pass road closures, perhaps by dismounting for a short distance. This is convenient and can often provide more pleasant and quieter riding conditions for a short while.

It is a gamble to ignore a closure sign if you don't know what lies ahead. Ask a local if they know what the closure is, or look on a map, sat nav or 3G phone app for where the road may be closed. A damaged bridge or new road under construction may be impassable, otherwise, you will probably be able to get through on a bicycle.

RIDER CHECKLIST

- **Treat all roadworks you come across as hazards.**
- **If the road is narrowed, ride as you would on a road of similar width, but allow for the possibility of surface damage.**
- **Expect to be able to pass temporary road closures unless there is reason to think otherwise.**
- **Do not ride against the flow on a road signed for one-way working.**

Cycling for the whole family

Teaching children to cycle safely is time well spent, and it guarantees great days out for the whole family

Cycling is a great activity for all the family, both as individuals and when riding together.

Children really enjoy cycling, which can help greatly to foster their development as individuals. Parents too, will find that cycling together adds another dimension to family life, everyone participating together in an activity that is not only good for health and fitness, but to which can be added the fascination and excitement of exploration.

Parents should ride with their child on the road as soon as they can

There are many options for children to accompany their parents by bicycle.
Babies can be carried in a sling, strapped to the parent's chest.

Child trailers can be fitted with a baby carrier and then, as the child grows, they can sit in it, secured with a harness.

When children can sit up unsupported, they can be carried in a child seat fitted to a parent's cycle. Buy a seat with straps – to secure the child at both the waist and shoulders – and a full back and headrest. Make sure that the child's feet are clear of the wheel and other moving parts.

Putting a child into and out of a child seat takes care. Ensure the bicycle is well supported and never let go of it at any point while the child is in the seat. Do not count on a flip-down cycle stand to support the bike with a child in its seat. Getting on and off the bike with a child seated also takes practice. Holding the handlebar firmly, bend your leg more at the knee and 'step' over the crossbar.

When riding, be prepared for the unpredictable movement of the child, and allow for the extra weight when starting and stopping. Use a lower gear than when riding by yourself.

When a child is too big for a child seat, a trailer-cycle can be bought that fixes to the back of a parent's bike. The trailer-cycle has its own handlebar and pedals for the child to use and may also have its own gears. Riding with a trailer-cycle is more difficult due to its weight and high fixing point. Be particularly careful on corners or the bike/trailer combination may jack-knife. Trailer-cycles can be used until about the age of 10.

One of the best ways for children to learn about cycling and to develop road skills is by riding as 'stoker' on the back of a tandem. This can be done from about three-years old using 'kiddy cranks' and later without them. The child will enjoy 'pedalling' when they are able and at other times their legs will spin harmlessly as their parent does the work.

How to be a better cyclist

RIDING ALONE

From the age of three or four, children can ride their own bike. Try to avoid the use of stabiliser wheels which can delay a child learning to balance. Instead, support your child's bike from behind with your hand under the saddle while they learn to counteract falling to one side by steering in the same direction. Most children pick this up quickly. Children should be taught good cycling practice from day one, introducing new skills as their ability allows. Always be positive to your child about cycling. Address the very limited risks through the encouragement of safe cycling techniques, not by engendering fear or by being over-protective.

It is very important that children are equipped, through training, to cycle on road as

soon as possible and that pavement cycling is then discouraged. Pavements are seldom safe places to cycle and lead to bad habits that can result in injury. Children are safer on the roads, once they have acquired the basic skills.

CYCLING WITH CHILDREN

The best way to teach your children to cycle well is by example. If you have acquired the skills of advanced cycling, you are ideally placed to pass those skills on to your children.

At as early an age as possible, introduce your children to cycling on roads. First on quiet, local roads and then, as their confidence and skills increase, take them onto roads with more traffic. Increase the difficulty of the route gradually. For example, start using busy roads by turning left on and left off. Make your first trips on main roads when traffic is light. As far as possible, keep to routes where the risks are manageable; dismounting to avoid difficult places can create negative associations between cycling and traffic that are unhelpful to a child's progress.

You should normally ride behind a child and at first slightly to the right, staying within hearing distance. Move further left when the child is able to look behind. Through junctions, ride alongside the child, usually on the right, to give reassurance and protection.

If both parents ride with their children, one should lead the way, to show where to ride, the other should stay at the back, coming alongside only at junctions. Keep close to one another so that the group is not split up.

RIDER CHECKLIST
- Always be positive to children about cycling – do not exaggerate the risks.
- Start cycling when children are young; always set a good example for them to follow.
- Make sure that your child's bike is the right size, properly adjusted and regularly maintained. These are parental responsibilities.
- Ride on the roads with your children as soon as possible.
- Gradually increase the difficulty of the roads on which you ride with your children.
- Support your children to continue cycling as teenagers.

Advanced Riding Index

A

Acceleration.............................26, 42
Advanced stop lines.................... 57

B

Basics.......................................12
Bicycle types...............................14
Blind spots...........................23, 31
Brake failure................................ 47
Brakes......................................44, 47
Braking......................................44
Braking, emergency...................46
Braking distance.........................45
Bus lanes....................................... 70

C

Cattle grids.................................. 79
Children.......................................88
Clothing......................................19
Cold weather................................82
Congestion..............................65, 71
Crossroads....................................56
Country bends.............................. 41
Country lanes 76
Countryside..................................75

Cycle facilities...............................72
Cycle lanes.................................57, 72
Cycle tracks (next to road)........73

D

Dazzle.. 81
Diversions 87
Driver reactions.........................74

F

Family cycling 88
Filtering.. 65
Filtering, common errors 67
Filtering, undertaking.................68
Fog and mist 82
Fords 79
Forward clearance 46
Forward observation....................31
Forward vision 40

G

Gears.......................................26, 48

H

Hazards...................................10, 24

Helmets 23
Hills...77
Horses 79

I

Information....................................26
IAM products and services 95
IPSGA 26, 51

J

Junctions 40, 50

L

Left turn 40, 51
Limit point of vision....................78
Looking behind 31

M

Main roads (in countryside) 75
Maintenance checklist 16
Mini-roundabouts.........................53
Momentum, conservation of ...42

N

Negotiation....................................58

Nightime cycling..........................80

O

Observation..........................30, 65
Overtaking..................................59

P

Planned system of riding..........26
Positioning.................................38
Primary position........................38

R

Rain 82
Reaction distances.....................13
Reaction times...........................13
Rear observation........................31
Riding plans...............................36
Riding position 23
Right turn................27, 40, 56, 60
Road signs 34
Road surfaces.......................32, 69
Roadworks.................................86
Roundabouts 52, 62

S

Secondary position 38
Selective observation.................32
Signalling...................................26
Signalling at roundabouts 54
Skidding....................................45
Snow and ice.............................83
Speed..26
Standard riding positions..........38
Stepping stones.........................66
Stopping distance 45
Summer cycling..........................84

T

T-junctions 40, 56
Towns...................................41, 64
Traffic lights.............................. 57
Turning 40

U

Undertaking 68

W

Wind 82

www.iam.org.uk

Thank you

The IAM would like to thank the following people and organisations
for their assistance in creating this book:

Cyclists:
Richard Cooper: Cycle Instructor
Steve Allsopp: Cycle Instructor
Sue Flower: Cycle Instructor
Claire Maxted: Cycling enthusiast
Oliver Laverack: Cycling enthusiast
Samuel Oakley: Cycling enthusiast
Hayley: Cover model

For the loan of equipment:
Halfords Cycle Superstore, Peterborough
Richardsons Cycle Shop, Queensgate, Peterborough
Trek and Giant cycles

The Institute of Advanced Motorists (IAM) is a road-safety charity that offers a wide range of information, advice, training and testing for road users.

The IAM delivers comprehensive training for car, HGV, PSV and company car drivers. It also provides in-depth training and testing for motorcyclists, as well as training, advice and information for cyclists.

Training is provided in several formats, from paid-for, one-to-one tuition with professional trainers, to unpaid drive-outs with trained volunteer observers.

A nationwide network of passionate IAM driving and motorcycling groups, provides the basis for the volunteer training, and most towns and cities have a group.

Check out the IAM's website at www.iam.org.uk for more information on your nearest group and a full list of services and information on offer from the organisation.

OTHER IAM PRODUCTS AND SERVICES

Advanced Driving

Thousands of drivers take our Advanced Driving programme (Skill for Life) every year. Their feedback is impressive - they find the experience enjoyable, the observing excellent, and often say it is one of the best things they have ever done. Many also go on to receive substantially reduced motor insurance premiums.

So, let the Institute of Advanced Motorists improve your technique and safety, increase your ability and confidence behind the wheel, and, ultimately, help you to get the most out of the total driving experience.

Advanced Motorcycling

If you're passionate about motorcycling, let us help to give your skills a boost, improve your technique and get the most out of the whole riding experience.

The Advanced Motorcycling programme (Skill for Life) also helps improve your road safety.

But that's not all. Like any positive learning experience, it has many benefits. Being safer is just the start, we also offer fantastic skills and track days, delivering greater confidence and enhanced enjoyment.

The IAM are fully-committed to helping make you a better motorcycle rider.

IAM Observer/Senior Observer

If you really want to make the best use of your excellent, newly-acquired driving or riding skills, the way forward is to consider helping others to become Advanced Motorists.

The IAM is always looking for new volunteers and observers to help deliver its Advanced programmes. You can be part of this scheme, by joining the IAM group network as a volunteer observer.

For further information, or to find your local IAM Group, visit www.iam.org.uk

Notes

Notes

IAM Contact Details
IAM, IAM House, 510 Chiswick High Road, London. W4 5RG

Tel: 0208 996 9600
E-Mail: enquiries@iam.org.uk
Web: www.iam.org.uk